# Praise for books by Paris Permenter & John Bigley

"The husband-and-wife team of Paris Permenter and John Bigley have been the most prolific travel writers in the state."—*Austin Chronicle*

"Paris and John know their territory well..."—*Southern Living*

"Visitors will find this book a terrific resource..."—*Family Travel Times*

"...*Texas Barbecue* is a highly recommended addition to any kitchen cookbook shelf..."—*Midwest Book Review*

"If you're looking for a one- or two-day getaway but you're not sure where to go, then Paris Permenter and John Bigley may have just the ticket for you." —*Hill Country News*

"Getaways for two run the gamut...all readily available in Texas, as you'll find in a new guidebook by travel writers Paris Permenter and John Bigley."—*The Dallas Morning News*

"*Texas Barbecue* was written by a couple of the best Texas writers around, Paris Permenter and John Bigley..."—*Houston Post*

"After logging 8,000 miles, Austinites Paris Permenter and John Bigley know the high roads and the back roads of Central and South Texas." —*Austin American-Statesman*

"...an ideal reference tool for the aficionado of good food and high-quality accommodations." —*Library Journal*

"In Texas, barbecue is a religion. So when authors Paris Permenter and John Bigley made a pilgrimage to the Barbecue Belt..., they were inspired to write *Texas Barbecue*..."—*Texas Monthly*

"...boasts the beef on the state's best barbecue pits..."—*Texas Highways*

## Also by Paris Permenter & John Bigley

*Adventure Guide to the Cayman Islands* (Hunter Publishing)
*Adventure Guide to Jamaica* (Hunter Publishing)
*Adventure Guide to the Leeward Islands* (Hunter Publishing)
*The Alamo City Guide* (Two Lane)
*Antigua, Barbuda, St. Kitts and Nevis Alive!* (Hunter Publishing)
*Caribbean for Lovers* (Prima)
*Caribbean with Kids* (Open Road)
*Cayman Islands Alive!* (Hunter Publishing)
*CitySmart: Austin* (Avalon)
*Day Trips from Austin* (Globe Pequot)
*Day Trips from San Antonio* (Globe Pequot)
*Fodor's In Focus Jamaica* (Random House)
*Fodor's Pocket Jamaica* (Random House)
*Gourmet Getaways* (Callawind)
*Insiders' Guide to San Antonio* (Globe Pequot)
*Jamaica Alive!* (Hunter Publishing)
*Las Vegas with Kids* (Open Road)
*Nassau and the Best of the Bahamas Alive!* (Hunter Publishing)
*National Parks with Kids* (Open Road)
*Romantic Getaways in the Caribbean* (Hunter Publishing)
*San Antonio in Your Pocket* (Globe Pequot)
*A Taste of the Bahamas* (Hunter Publishing)
*A Taste of Jamaica* (Hunter Publishing)
*Texas Barbecue* (Two Lane)
*Texas Getaways for Two* (Two Lane)

# Barkonomics:

## Tips for Frugal Fidos

**By Paris Permenter & John Bigley**

**Founders of DogTipper.com**

## Visit us online!

### For updates, more resources, and suggestions for the next edition,

### visit DogTipper.com

## Disclaimer

This book has been written to provide information to help you save money on your dog's care and live a better life with your dog. The purpose of this book is to educate and entertain. The authors and publisher shall have neither liability nor responsibility to any person or entity with respect to any loss or damage caused or alleged to be caused directly or indirectly by this book.

This book in no way replaces specific advice from your veterinarian. If you have any concerns at all about your dog's health, please make an appointment with your vet, and have him examined by a professional. If you do not wish to be bound by the above, please return this book for a full refund.

# Table of Contents

# Introduction

In 2008, we adopted two young rescue dogs, Irie, in February, and Tiki, in August. In late August, we launched a website featuring tips for dog lovers, DogTipper.com. We had been publishing travel websites since 2000 but we decided we'd like to focus on something closer to home this time since travel wasn't all it used to be. We took a look at the two sweet faces of our dogs, and we had our topic.

A couple of months later, travel wasn't the only industry taking a steep step back; the whole world was cinching up its economic belts in the face of financial freefall.

Suddenly frugal wasn't cheap. It was smart. It was necessary.

Not that we hadn't been on the frugal bandwagon for a long, long time. After Paris graduated from college with double degrees in Economics and Accounting (followed by graduate school, then a few years of teaching Economics), we launched our writing business with a slim budget. Self-employment requires some strict discipline when it comes to the dollar.

Since we've always lived with multiple dogs and cats, we've perpetually had the household budget on a short leash by necessity. Through the years, we've faced rising pet product prices and veterinary costs. In the last two decades, we also had to work some serious pet health expenditures into that budget: Yoda's cancer treatments, removal of Kit Kat's brain tumor, Elaine's heart disease and lifelong medication, Alby's epilepsy testing and lifelong medication, Hershey's thyroid testing and medication as she grew older, Cheeto's and Snickers's urinary tract problems, Shady's fall from our second floor office window down into our bedroom that resulted in back problems for the remainder of her life. They each took a toll on our hearts—and on our budget—but that's how it is with family. You do what you have to do and what you can do.

So, like so many people, when a tight budget we'd already been living and working under grew even tighter in 2008, we started trimming. And we discovered that there were plenty of ways we could cut household expenses—including our dog expenditures—and still enjoy the same standard of living. Using smart shopping techniques, a little research, and, in some cases, a little more elbow grease, we could give our dogs the same good quality food, the same preventative care, and the same amount of comfort and fun.

As our DogTipper.com site grew, we heard from more and more people who were also looking for ways to cut their pet expenditures. We also learned about the increase in economic euthanizations, instances where pet lovers were faced with the heartbreaking decision to euthanize a pet because necessary veterinary treatment could not be afforded. We heard of the sad increase in owner surrenders and abandonment due to unemployment, foreclosure, and extreme financial hardships.

Soon, the idea for *Barkonomics* was born.

We've aimed this book at all income levels and for people with one dog or, like us, with many pets. We hope this book can help dog lovers:

- Who are trying to cut costs so they'll be able to keep their pets and avoid surrendering them to a shelter or rehoming them.

- Who are hoping to trim dog costs so they'll be able to live more comfortably in all aspects of their life.

- Who are looking for ways to cut expenditures so they can afford veterinary care for their dog or are looking for alternative ways to finance that medical help.

- Who are looking for ways to trim costs so they can stretch their pet dollars and make room for an additional pet in their home.

- Who would like to pamper their pets by using smart shopping techniques that allow them to make either extra purchases or higher quality purchases for their dog.

Along the way, we've interviewed numerous experts in all areas of dog care for their ideas and tips on stretching your dog dollars. We've surveyed DogTipper.com readers to learn about the ways they'd like to cut costs. And we've talked with fellow dog lovers we found everywhere from dog festivals to dog parks to our local grocery store about how they're making the most of their pet purchasing power.

We've learned a lot. For all our longtime frugal ways, we've picked up some new techniques including some high-tech ways to save in this Internet age.

And we've been reminded of a very important lesson that our dogs teach us every day: the best things in life are free. From that extra-long walk to another game of fetch, the time you and your dog spend together is the best gift of all for your faithful friend!

# Keeping an Eye on Fido's Finances

In today's tough economic times, everyone has an eye on the budget and that includes expenditures for dog food, supplies, and care. However, with a little preparation, research, and even some home cooking, you can continue to make your dog's life as rich as ever while saving money at the same time!

Not that there's not plenty of temptation to spend those bucks on Bowser; the pet industry is enormous, fetching $45.5 billion per year and growing at a rate of about $2 billion per year. According to the American Pet Products Association (APPA), the biggest share, nearly $18 billion, goes to the pet food industry, followed by veterinary care, supplies and over the counter medications, pet services (grooming and boarding), and finally live animal purchases.

The booming pet industry can unleash real savings for the frugal shopper, though. With many companies still entering the market, competition is fierce. And competition spells opportunity for shoppers! Coupons, free samples, special discounts, loyalty programs, and other sales techniques give you the chance to try more pet products and save money at the same time.

Pet lovers are definitely trying to save money these days, cutting their dog-related expenses in several areas. A recent survey of 1,000 members of the American Kennel Club showed that:

- 52 percent look for sales and/or clip coupons before shopping for pet products

- 48 percent are purchasing fewer toys/treats and other non-essential dog supplies

The poll started us wondering about how DogTipper readers were watching their doggie dollars. While only about 28 percent of DogTipper readers were presently clipping coupons, we found that they're definitely seeking ways to cut costs. Over 55 percent say they've comparison shopped to find the best prices on dog items. Nearly half of those surveyed said they'd love to find ways to trim veterinary expenses while nearly a third would like to reduce pet medication costs.

Cutting costs in all those categories—and more—is possible with a little extra effort. Surprisingly, some of that effort isn't even all that time-consuming; some of it just means making different choices, shopping with an eye for bargains, and setting priorities to recognize what's worth the expenditure—and what's not.

# The Cost of Living with a Dog

Just how much does it cost to have a dog? The cost varies based on many factors: where you get your dog, your dog's breed and size, the lifestyle you provide your dog, and where you live. Let's face it: some geographic areas have a higher cost of living and that extends to pets as well.

# Obtaining Your Dog

The cost of obtaining Fido is just the first expense you'll have over the lifetime of your dog. It's simple to compare the purchase price of those "free puppies" in your neighborhood to the show quality dog from a breeder with a price tag that can run into the thousands but, when you take into account the many expenses you'll incur later, it's easy to see that no dog is "free."

## *Shelters*

The most economical place to get a dog is a local shelter where you'll be saving a life and gaining a new best friend. Both of our dogs, along with many of our previous dogs, came from area shelters; shelters are our number one destination when it comes to adding to our family.

Although fees and services vary from location to location, for about a $100 donation you can adopt a dog who usually has been spayed or neutered, received a health check, often been microchipped, and received shots appropriate for his age. When you look at everything the shelter donation includes, you'll see it's a far more economical choice than that "free" dog your neighbors might be offering.

Let's do the math:

**Value of shelter services:**

- o Spay or neuter: $150-$250 (depending on size, sex of dog)
- o First year of shots $150
- o Microchipping $50
- o Deworming $30

**Total:** $380-$480

This savings doesn't include other veterinary care the dog may have received, heartworm preventative, flea preventative, etc.

Let's compare the cost of adoption to the services you'll receive:

> Value of shelter services received: $380-$480
> Minus adoption fee: $100 (this varies)
>
> **Your savings:** $280-$380

Now, compare that to what you'd spend for a dog from a breeder or pet store:

> Average cost of purebred dog: $800 (or higher)
> Cost of spaying/neutering: $150-$250
> Total: $950-$1050 (or higher)
>
> Compared to shelter adoption fee: $100 (this varies)
>
> **Amount you save by adopting instead of purchasing from a breeder or pet store:** $850-$950 (or higher)

When you do the math, you'll see that the shelter dog is a bargain!

In addition, some shelters offer a free first month of pet insurance; one of those free policies was a big help to us when we adopted our dog Irie. She had demodectic mange when we brought her home. The insurance paid for her treatments over the coming months (we paid the insurance premiums after that free first month). In all, we had very few out of pocket costs for her dips and skin scrapes over the course of her treatment.

You'll find many mixed breed dogs (our favorite!) at shelters and you will also find specific breeds. Did you know that, according to statistics from The National Council on Pet Population, Study and Policy, about one-fourth of the dogs in shelters are purebred dogs?

To search for a particular breed of dog in your area, visit *www.petfinder.com*. This site allows you to search by zip code, breed, gender, and more. Another good option is *www.AdoptAPet.com*.

## Saving on Shelter Adoptions

Many shelters offer discounted rates on senior pets throughout the year (and especially during November, which is Adopt a Senior Pet Month). Adopting an older dog can be a money-saver since you'll avoid puppy problems like chewing and you might get a pre-trained dog.

Shelter dogs will have received shots appropriate for their age but generally you'll find that puppies still need additional shots (at your expense) after their adoption. Young puppies are sometimes too young to have been spayed or neutered as well.

Senior dogs, on the other hand, will be current on their shots from the shelter and generally will have been spayed and neutered. Consider this savings when weighing the cost of potential health costs (such as arthritis medication) for an older dog.

Some shelters also offer occasional "markdowns" on adult dogs, dogs that have been at the shelter a long time, black dogs (which, due to a phenomenon known as "Black Dog Syndrome," often have a tough time getting adopted), dogs with physical challenges, etc.

## *Rescues*

If your heart is set on a particular breed, look to breed rescues. (You'll also find other types of rescues such as small dog rescues, hound rescues, etc.) Like a shelter, rescues are both an economical choice and one that's saving a life. Breed rescues are operated by loving breed experts; they take in homeless dogs of that particular breed and find them new homes. Some rescues have a central facility but many operate through a network of foster homes.

The cost of a dog from a rescue varies but, in general, expect to pay a cost of $200-$300. This will generally include spay/neuter, vaccinations appropriate for the dog's age, and an assessment of the dog's behavior and personality. Because these dogs are often fostered in private homes, rescues will usually be able to tell you more about the dog—and if he'll be a good fit for your family—than a crowded shelter would.

Recently, we interviewed David Frei, host of the annual Westminster Dog Show and National Dog Show, and asked him about an economical way to obtain a specific breed. "Every parent club like the Afghan Hound Club of America has a rescue body along with the parent club so that if you're interested in an Afghan Hound you can go to that parent club's Web page, look it up and find the rescue," said Frei.

celebrity tip

"A lot of dogs end up in rescues for the silliest of reasons or for the most tragic of reasons," continued Frei. "Sometimes, there's a death in the family or a divorce or somebody's moving or whatever, and there are silly reasons that they end up in rescues. You can get a perfectly good dog out of rescue." To find rescue clubs, visit *www.akc.org*.

In all, the cost of rescues come out far ahead of purebreds purchased from a breeder and offers an affordable way to add a particular breed to your family—and to save a life—at the same time.

## *"Free" Dogs*

One of the most popular methods for obtaining a new dog is getting a "free" dog from family or friends. Stray dogs with no home also become new pets. In the past, we've added to our own family both ways with Hershey, a Newfoundland/Springer Spaniel who joined our home when our daughter's teacher's dog had puppies, and with Alby, an Australian cattle dog that wandered up to our house and quickly found a home in our hearts.

While these dogs seem "free," be sure to realize that no dog is free. Expect to spend about $150 for that first year of puppy shots (your puppy will have three rounds of shots) and about $150-$250 to spay/neuter depending on your vet and the size and sex of your dog.

## *Breeders*

If you're going to a breeder to find your new dog, don't try to save money on this step. Lower cost "backyard breeders" and pet stores (which most often get their dogs from puppy mills) may have puppies whose heritage isn't known so you don't have the benefit of testing for potentially expensive hereditary problems such as hip dysplasia. (And don't even let us get started on the horrible, inhumane conditions at puppy mills and why you shouldn't support these mills through your purchase of a puppy.)

Instead, look for a reputable dog breeder who will have worked to maintain the highest standards of the breed to produce healthy puppies. To find a reputable breeder in your area, check the American Kennel Club website, *www.akc.org*, for the AKC Breeder Referral page. Talk with club members for their recommendations. Dog shows can also be a great opportunity to talk with breeders and meet professionals dedicated to making the breed the best it can be.

When you believe you've found a good breeder, go just a little further and check on the business history of that breeder. Check with the American Kennel Club on any past complaints; call the AKC Customer Service at (919) 233-9767 or email *Info@akc.org*. Also, check with your local Better Business Bureau, *www.bbb.org*, for past or pending problems.

The cost of a dog from a breeder will vary by breed and location but expect to pay between $500 and $2000 for most breeds (higher for hard-to-find breeds) with an average price running about $800.

Puppies are often divided into "show quality" dogs and lower-priced "pet quality" dogs, which breeders require to be spayed or neutered because it doesn't exhibit the strict characteristics of a show dog.

When you buy a puppy from a breeder, you should expect to receive:

- Your dog's pedigree or "papers." The words "American Kennel Club" as well as the AKC logo should be clearly visible. You'll need to send in this application form to register your dog with the AKC. The AKC warns that you should be wary of a breeder who refuses or hesitates to give you these papers, wants to charge you more for AKC papers, offers papers from a registry other than the AKC, or tells you he will mail them to you at a later date.

- Your dog's pedigree for three or more generations.

- Proof that his hips and his elbows have been certified as "good" or "excellent" by the OFA or Orthopedic Foundation for Animals.

- Certification from the Canine Eye Registration Foundation (CERF) that his eyes are free of genetic abnormalities.

# Making a Decision

When making a decision of which dog to add to your family, it's easy to go with your heart—not your pocketbook. However, you can ask yourself some financial and lifestyle questions to narrow your decision *before* you begin your search for a dog:

- **Do I want a small or large dog?** In the next section, we'll compare the cost of living with a small dog versus a large dog. Although size doesn't greatly impact expenses such as veterinary bills, size does matter when it comes to the food bill. If you don't already have a dog and you're not familiar with dog food prices, do some preliminary research before you make a decision on the size of dog you'd like to add to your family. Go to a pet supply store and check prices for high-quality dog food.

- **Do I want a long- or short-haired dog?** Some dog breeds will require frequent, regular grooming. You can learn grooming skills but, if you don't think you have the time or inclination to learn dog grooming, you'll need to take your dog to a professional groomer. If you don't want to add this expense to your dog budget, just opt for a short-haired dog.

- **Will my dog's breed impact my homeowner's or renter's insurance?** Some insurance companies will not cover certain breeds of dogs in the liability clauses of your homeowner's insurance, meaning you'll need to get an additional insurance policy. (If you live in Ohio, you are required to have a minimum of $100,000 liability insurance if you have what they deem a pit bull-type dog.) Typically the dog breeds included in these insurance restrictions are "bully breeds" and very powerful breeds: Akitas, Alaskan Malamutes, American Pit Bull Terriers, American Staffordshire Terrier, American Bulldogs, Boxers, Chow Chows, Doberman Pinschers, German Shepherds, Great

Danes, Presa Canarios, Rottweilers, Siberian Huskies, Wolf hybrids, and others. If you need to buy a separate rider to cover your dog, it can cost $1,000 per year.

As you're making these decisions, also take a good, honest look at your lifestyle: your home, the outdoor space you have to offer that dog (and whether it is fenced), and your own activity level.

Before a recent National Dog Show, we interviewed actor John O'Hurley who, besides his well-known role in "Seinfeld," is also a dog lover, author of dog books, and the host of the National Dog Show television broadcast. According to O'Hurley:

celebrity
tip

> "I think the first thing that you have to do is to find a dog that fits your lifestyle, and I think you have to be very, very honest about what you have to offer a dog rather than what the dog has to offer you.

> Nothing distresses me more than to see a Great Dane walking out of a small apartment in New York City, you know it just doesn't fit. It's, I think, a certain sense of irresponsibility in that you have to really give the dog what it needs in an environment. I think that the first part of responsible dog ownership is to find a dog that meets your ability to maintain that dog."

## Startup Costs

After the cost of obtaining your dog, let's look at other start up expenses.

The ASPCA has issued some good guidelines on dog costs, estimating the costs during a time when you'll have spay/neuter costs, training classes, purchasing a crate, etc. Their estimates are:

Small dog  $470
Medium dog  $565
Large dog  $560

Why, you ask (as did we), would it be cheaper to make purchases for a large dog than a medium dog? They allow $60 for a carrier bag for a medium-sized dog but no carrier bag for a large dog.

The cost of what you really need to start off your new puppy or dog varies by your plans for life with your dog (do you plan to travel with your dog? where will he sleep?), your shopping skills, and your willingness to shop for used items and great bargains. Here's our list of your dog's "starter kit," items you need when you bring that new dog home:

- **Collars or harness.** We recommend a collar for everyday wear that contains your dog tag and a separate collar (or harness) for the walk. We use a quick release collar for everyday wear and we bought the cheapest we could find when the dogs were in their chewing phase and literally chewed the collars off each other. (Cost: $3-5 each) For walking, we use Martingale collars, ones that tighten if the dog tries to back out but can't tighten and choke your dog like a slip collar. (Cost: $6-12)

- **Dog tag.** Our Walmart has a tag making machine and can include four lines of personalization; a tag costs $4-5.

- **Leash.** We recommend purchasing a good leash that you'll be happy with for a long time. Along with a leash that's comfortable in your hands, you want one that's secure for you to hold (we like a loop we can put a hand through then wrap for a good hold, NOT a retractable leash with a plastic grip.) We purchased leather leashes for about $15 each; they're comfortable and strong, even with our 70-pound dog on the other end.

- **Dog Food.** Dog food is another item where you want to shop for quality. Premium dog food runs about $15-$18 per 4- to 6-pound bag.

- **Dog Bed.** You can easily make your own dog bed using discarded clothing and linens around the house (see our Dog Supplies section for ideas). Cost: free; $15-30 for inexpensive purchased bed.

- **Dog house.** If your dog will be spending much time outdoors, you'll need to supply a good dog house that will provide protection from the elements. Search Freecycle and Craigslist and you might find one for free; if purchased, expect to spend anywhere from $30-$80, depending on size (and more if you get fancy).

- **Crate**. Crate training can help speed housetraining of young dogs and provide your dog with his own special, safe place within your home. Again, you can find crates on Freecycle and Craigslist as well as thrift shops if you keep looking; if new, expect to spend $30-$130, depending on size.

- **Bowls**. You'll need a bowl for food and a bowl for water (and we recommend two for each so you can wash them more frequently). We've purchased all of ours at thrift shops for $1-$2 each.

- **Toys.** Our dogs absolutely love toys and have many (OK, we admit: too many) toys that we've picked up for as little as 25 cents at garage sales and thrift stores.

## Year-to-Year Costs

Beyond your "startup" costs, your annual costs will also vary by the size of your dog, largely because of food costs.

For your annual costs, the ASPCA estimates:

Small dog: $580
Medium dog: $695
Large dog: $875

Just how those annual expenditures break down varies from home to home, of course, but, in general, the biggest difference in the annual cost of small versus large dogs comes in the category of food. The ASPCA estimates a small dog will cost $55 per year to feed, a medium dog $120, and a large dog will cost $235 per year to feed.

We'll show you ways we save on those dog food expenses (both our dogs fall in the large dog category) with everything from coupons to supplementing their diet with homemade food.

Remember, though, that your dog food expense is one area where you don't want to cut too many corners; we never buy cheap food (premium food bought cheaply is another story!) Premium dog food containing quality ingredients is an investment in your dog's health that saves you money down the line.

There are plenty of other places where you can cut corners, though. The American Pet Products Association asks pet owners every year just how they spend their dollars. According to the latest APPA National Pet Owners Survey, dog owners spend quite a bit more than the ASPCA estimates above.

Here are the APPA survey results:

| Surgical Vet Visits | $532 |
|---|---|
| Food | $229 |
| Kennel Boarding | $273 |
| Routine Vet | $225 |
| Groomer/Grooming Aids | $66 |

| | |
|---|---|
| Vitamins | $61 |
| Food Treats | $64 |
| Toys | $40 |

Categories that don't impact your dog's health—like toys and, in many cases, grooming—are areas ripe for some budgetary trimming.

Like all areas of your financial life, there are ways to trim both startup and recurring costs—without sacrificing the health or happiness of your dog. And that's what this book is all about!

# Food and Treats

Aside from veterinary costs associated with potential accidents or health issues with your dog, the cost of food and treats is your top recurring expenditure. Fortunately, since it represents such a large portion of your pet care budget, food is also an area where it's possible to realize cost savings.

No, we're *not* talking about finding the cheapest dog food on the market. After all, like the saying goes, "You are what you eat" –and that axiom holds true for your dog as well. High quality food is an investment in your dog's health.

How then to realize those savings? Read on for ways to save while keeping Rover—not fat and happy—but well-fed, healthy, and happy!

# Learn to read labels.

Price doesn't necessarily equal quality. To get the best dog food you can afford, take the time to read the labels. Look for meat—and a *specific* kind of meat like lamb, chicken, or beef, not "animal by-products" with no species listed.

On the dog food package, items are listed by weight, starting with the most used ingredient in the food. That specific kind of meat should be the first ingredient. Also, look for whole fruits and vegetables and whole grains. Corn is typically used as inexpensive filler; better foods will have higher quality grains such as brown rice, rolled oats, barley, quinoa, and millet.

It pays to take the time to read those labels and select good food for your dog. The price difference between high and low quality food isn't as steep as you might think: your dog does not need to be fed as much high-quality food as he would low-quality food packed with fillers.

## Finding Coupons

*Yes, coupon clipping is an oldie but a goodie method for saving money...but with some high-tech twists these days. Coupons can save you money on dog food, dog treats, cleaning supplies, and staples you're purchasing to make your own dog food.*

*Coupon codes can save you money on items you're ordering online for your dog: bedding, leashes, crates, and more.*

**Clip those Sunday newspaper coupons.**

The Sunday newspaper remains a popular source for dog food and dog treat coupons. Every week (holiday weekends are the exception) you'll find coupon inserts from the major coupon companies: Red Plum (*www.redplum.com*), Smart Source (*www.smartsource.com*), and, less frequently, Proctor &Gamble (*www.pgeverydaysolutions.com*).

If you find some exceptional coupons, buy another copy of the paper (or ask friends and family to save you theirs)—it can definitely pay for itself several times over!

**Search for dog-related coupons online.**

Before you head to the grocery store, do an online check for coupons at *www.couponmom.com, www.coolsavings.com, www.wow-coupons.com* (with US and UK coupons), *www.coupons.com* and others. Usually you'll need to download a printer application that permits you to print coupons.

Once you print the coupons, don't cut them out but instead take in the entire page to your store so they can see you didn't copy the coupons but instead have printed a legitimate printable coupon. You can print the coupon in black ink (you'll save money by not printing in color.)

special tip

*If you have questions about using printable coupons, check your store's coupon policy on the store website; most spell out their policy toward printables. (Generally most grocery stores accept printable coupons that include a bar code.)*

**Sit up and beg.**

As you've probably learned from your dog by now, it never hurts to ask! Try sending a nice email to your favorite dog-related companies (see Appendix A for a list of websites for some of the largest) and requesting coupons or coupon codes. Many companies will supply coupons on request to faithful (or potential) customers.

**Look for a manufacturer's coupons on its website.**

If your dog especially loves a particular brand of dog food, visit the manufacturer's website for potential coupons and offers. You'll often find downloadable coupons (especially if they're coming out with a new product.) Again, check Appendix A for a list of websites where you can begin your coupon quest.

**Sign up for newsletters for favorite companies.**

Many dog food and treat manufacturers offer electronic newsletters that provide special discounts and coupons, news of new products, and subscriber-only specials. Check their websites for signups.

special tip

*Create a special email address on Yahoo, Google, Hotmail or another free service. Reserve this address just for your dog-related emails such as coupon requests and newsletter subscriptions.*

**Follow favorites on Twitter and Facebook.**

Just about every company has a Twitter and Facebook presence these days (just check the company website for links). You'll often find some great fan/follower discount offers that are only promoted through Twitter and Facebook; we've received and redeemed some good discount codes for everything from bully sticks to dog toys this way.

*When we find dog-related special offers on Facebook and Twitter, we publish links to them on our Twitter account, @dogtipper, and our Facebook fan page, www.facebook.com/dogtipper.*

**Watch for Catalina coupons.**

Catalina coupons are printed on the back of the cash register tape when you check out at the grocery store. These coupon offers are usually matched to item categories you've just been shopping for so if you've been buying pet products, see if your Catalinas are also for related products!

The policy on Catalinas varies from store to store; we asked ours the other day why we didn't receive them every time we checked out (which we used to) and the checker explained that they only print out every so often. Sort of a coupon slot machine…

**Watch for peelies.**

Peelies are coupons that are stuck directly on the product itself. Even though they're affixed right on the product, don't expect the cashier to be keeping an eye out for them and pull them when you check out.

If the peelie is for that product, we pull the peelies as soon as the merchandise goes in our cart and add the coupon to our stack to turn in! If the peelie is for a future purchase, we pull and add to our coupon stash.

**Look for hang tags.**

Look for hang tags containing a coupon; the hang tag literally hangs around the neck of the product. They're often used on cleaning supplies…which, as a dog lover, you know you'll need.

**Watch for blinkies.**

Blinkies are coupons that are ejected by a blinking coupon dispenser attached to the shelf that holds the product. You won't find them everywhere but, when you do find them, be sure to grab a coupon to use this trip or the next time you're shopping.

**Look for tear pads.**

Tear pads, literally a pad of coupons, are easy to miss as you rush through the grocery store but they hang on the shelf usually below the appropriate item. It's OK to get a coupon to use that day and one for your next visit. (Ripping a bunch from the pad and leaving too few for the next shoppers is considered wrong, though…sort of like a dog scarfing up all his food then trying to get his buddy's food. Just don't or growling could ensue…)

**Look for in-store coupon booklets or circulars.**

Grocery stores and drugstores often print their own flyers with special in-store coupons. Look for these flyers near the store's main door. (A great thing about these in-store coupons: they can often be combined with a manufacturer's coupon for the same product to maximize your savings!)

We always grab a flyer as soon as we walk in the store and take a moment to flip through it to see if it includes any products on our shopping list.

**Get coupons downloaded to your phone.**

Applications like Coupon Sherpa (*www.couponsherpa.com*) can download coupons directly to your iPhone. You'll find online coupons, coupon codes, and printable coupons on the site. And just how do you redeem that coupon? Just show your phone to the cashier for scanning directly from the phone!

**Start your own coupon club.**

You're looking for dog-related coupons but do you have some friends who are seeking baby coupons? Or cat-related coupons? Start your own trading club! Another fun idea is a coupon party where you get together with friends and swap coupons.

# Using Coupons

*Long a favorite way to save money at the grocery store, you'll find that many other stores—pet supply stores, dollar stores, and drugstores—also accept coupons.*

**Learn about "stacking" coupons.**

Not all stores allow shoppers to "stack" coupons but, if yours does, it can be a real way to save. Here's how it works: if you have a manufacturer's coupon for Fido's Food and your store also offers its own coupon for Fido's Food, you can "stack" the two coupons to increase your savings.

This only works when one coupon is from the manufacturer and one from the store (you can't use two manufacturer's coupons on one sack of food…although you could buy two sacks of food with two coupons in most cases.)

**Save your coupons for a sale.**

We often notice that coupons run when there's a big push for that product, maybe because it's new, maybe because there's a seasonal tie-in. The same promotional efforts behind a coupon also go into putting the item on sale…so if you can wait to use your coupon until the item goes on sale, you'll stretch your savings even further!

To find out what's on sale at your local supermarket, check *www.couponmom.com* for a great database that matches local sales with coupons from the Sunday coupon supplements. All you do is save your supplements, and the database will tell you the date and coupon to grab. Another good reference site is *www.shoplocal.com* with weekly ads from local retailers.

**Ask about double coupon day.**

You'll still find some stores that offer a double (and, in rare cases, triple) coupon day but sometimes you have to ask to find out about it! It's definitely worth a call or a stop by the store's service desk on your next visit to ask.

**Learn your store's price matching policy.**

Does your grocery store have a price matching policy to match their competitor's sale price? Some stores do; check your store's website to see if you could be saving money with this policy. Usually a price matching policy requires that you bring in a flyer from their competitor that shows the lower price.

This can be a money-saver if you're buying a whole case of dog food and the per can price is even a few cents per can lower at a competing store. (You can, of course, always make a separate shopping trip to that second store…but that usually spells even more spending!)

**Ask if your store accepts competitor's store coupons.**

A similar way to save is to find out if your favorite store will accept store coupons from competing stores. These are coupons that are printed to be used within the store, not manufacturer's coupons. Again, check their website or stop by the service desk and ask!

**Find out about electronic coupon programs.**

A growing number of loyalty programs are offering e-coupons, loading electronic coupons onto your loyalty card so there are no coupons to clip. For example, the Randall's Remarkable Card and the Kroger's Plus Card allow you to go online and select coupons you'd like to load onto your card. When you check out at the store and swipe your loyalty card, you'll automatically be "turning in" the coupons.

Check other stores for this growing trend for e-coupons which have even hit warehouse clubs. For example, Sam's Club now offers eValues, a paperless coupon program for Advantage and Business members of the Sam's Club Plus® Membership. Members can check their offers online or at an in-store kiosk; also, the kiosk can send an eValues shopping list to the Member's iPhone, Blackberry, or smart phone.

**Use coupons at dollar stores.**

Did you know that many dollar stores accept manufacturer's coupons and some also have their own store coupons? Dollargeneral.com has printable store coupons on its website.

**Use coupons at drugstores.**

Shopping at drugstores is a saving method that's known to the most savvy shoppers. Did you know that Walgreens and CVS/pharmacy both accept coupons and offer savings programs? Both have pet sections, cleaning product sections, and pharmacies that offer many prescriptions written for dogs.

The ExtraCare card at CVS/pharmacy (*www.cvs.com*) earns two percent back on most purchases, money back on every two prescriptions filled (including pet prescriptions you can get filled at the pharmacy), provides coupons on your receipt, and offers "Extra Bucks" you can print and redeem.

Walgreens (*www.walgreens.com*) offers "Register Rewards," basically Catalina coupons that print out on your receipt for use on your future trips.

**Use coupons at pet supply stores.**

Don't forget to take your manufacturer's coupons with you to the pet supply stores! (And along with using coupons, be sure to use your loyalty card for extra savings and future discounts!)

**Search for local coupons.**

Most coupons found in newspaper supplements and at coupon sites are national in scope but one site, *www.CouponMap.com*, features local coupons. Enter your zip code to find coupons specific to your area; our recent search found local coupons for everything from a free veterinary visit to dog food discounts. Similarly, *www.valpak.com* is searchable by zip code (or city or state) offering coupons that range from grocery coupons to professional services such as grooming.

# Off to the Grocery Store

*Whether you're headed to the grocery store to buy dog food and cleaning supplies or meat and produce to make your own dog food and cleaners, basic savings techniques can trim your dog-related grocery costs.*

### Start a price book.

The idea behind a price book is to develop your ability to detect sales patterns and to help you identify a true sale price when you see one. We use a price book to track our favorite brands of dog food so we'll know when we come across the lowest price (then we'll know it's time to stock up!) A price book is simply a little notebook (or even index cards) with a list of the items you most commonly buy and the lowest price for each item.

Using a separate page (or card) for each product, make several columns: Date, Store, Size, Price, Unit Price. Fill in the information for the first four columns at the store or from your receipt once you return home.

Next, calculate the last column to determine the Unit Price—how much per pound is that dog food? This will be especially helpful in determining if larger sacks and purchases from membership clubs are a good bargain. Add the Unit Price to your page.

special tip

*Along with processed foods like dog food, a price book also helps you identify the right times and seasons for buying produce and meat if you're making your own dog food. It will also identify the sales patterns at your favorite stores. Many stores are on a six-week cycle for sale pricing popular*

*items. Look for sales on some meats and produce as holidays*
*approach or when produce is in season.*

**Search high and low shelves.**

The eye-level shelves at the grocery store contain the most
expensive and most promoted merchandise. By checking the
upper and lower shelves, you'll often find similar products at a
lower price! This holds true whether you're buying dog food and
supplies in the grocery store or the pet supply store.

**Shop with cash.**

Whether you're headed to the pet supply store or the grocery
store, go with a list, an estimated total, and cash in hand.

Avoiding ATMs, credit cards, and checkbooks help you keep an
eye on everything you pick up at the store—after all, no one
wants to be embarrassed by being short of money at checkout!
Shopping with cash will help you watch prices while you shop.

**Go in with a list in hand.**

We know that it's so, so easy to run into the store for a bag of
dog food...then suddenly that cute collar catches your eye. If you
go with a list of what you're buying firmly in hand, you're far
more likely to buy those items...and only those items.

Also, compiling that list before your store visit makes it much
easier to go ahead and pull the coupons for your purchases and
attach them to your list. (We know every time we take the whole
file of coupons with us, we get in a rush and run out of patience
matching purchase to coupon. Our favorite method is to write the
shopping list on an old envelope and put the appropriate coupons
inside the envelope!)

**Ask for a raincheck.**

When there's an advertised special, whether for dog biscuits or dog beds, and the store is out of stock, ask for a rain check.

# Cooking for Your Dog

*After the 2007 melamine recalls, a growing number of people began to prepare homemade dog food. Whether you go 100 percent homemade, supplement your dog's food with homemade food, or just prepare your own dog treats, you can shop carefully to save money. We supplement our dogs' kibble, cooking two crock pots of meat and veggies in the slow cooker per week, served alongside quality kibble at each meal. We also bake our own dog treats.*

**Make your own dog food.**

Making your own dog food can be a way to better control both cost and quality. It isn't difficult but it does require some preparation and savvy shopping to meet your dog's special needs. Talk with your veterinarian, invest in a good dog food cookbook (see below), and make the switch to homemade gradually to avoid disrupting your dog's digestive system.

**Invest in a good dog food cookbook.**

Making your dog's food isn't just a matter of whipping up a little extra food at every meal; you want to prepare food in the right proportions in terms of meats, vegetables, fruits, and carbohydrates.

Investing in a quality cookbook (or checking one out at your library) can provide recipes you rotate to keep your dog healthy and happy. A selection of recipes will also help your budget, allowing you to cook what's on sale that week. The time you spend studying recipes is well-spent since you'll keep your dog healthier and at a better weight.

*Looking for a good dog food cookbook? We like* The Whole Pet Diet: Eight Weeks to Great Health for Dogs and Cats *by Andi Brown.*

special tip

**Invest in a slow cooker.**

We love our slow cooker and purchased one just to make dog food. We bought ours on sale at the discount store, and it has paid for itself time and time again. (You can often buy slow cookers very cheaply at the thrift stores—this must be one appliance people get rid of because it's so large.)

Two nights a week, we toss in meat and vegetables and brown rice or other starch, simmering overnight. In the morning, we have dog food for the next three days to supplement the high-quality kibble (we feed half kibble, half homemade.) If you have smaller dogs (or just one dog) you'll need to cook less often.

**Watch for "last chance" fruits and meats.**

If you make your own dog food and treats, keep an eye out for the overripe fruits and vegetables on sale at your grocery store.

We check for these on every grocery store run and the other day we snagged an entire paper grocery bag of ripe bananas—seven hands of bananas—for just 99 cents! We peeled and froze the bananas to use in nutritious dog treats.

Similarly, you'll find meats that are sale priced because they've reached their "best by" date. These can be great low-cost items for your dog.

You'll want to use or freeze these purchases as soon as you get home.

**Shop farmers' markets.**

Buying directly from the farmer helps to cut out the costs that go into processing, packaging, distributing and ultimately displaying the product at a grocery store. Locally grown produce is also an eco-friendly choice that's delicious in addition to being inexpensive!

Also, you can save money by shopping a farmers' market at the end of the day when farmers want to move the last of their goods. Buy in bulk and you can increase that savings.

special tip

*Don't be afraid to ask farmers about bruised or damaged fruits and veggies they can't sell—often they're free for the asking (especially if you're making another purchase!)*

**Buy organ meats.**

The less desirable organ meats are inexpensive and make a good component to your dog's diet. Serving four or five percent organ meat in your dog's diet can benefit your pooch and your pocketbook. Our dogs love liver and kidneys.

Beef heart, which is a muscle meat, is another "less desirable" meat and easy on the budget (and the dogs are crazy about it!)

43

**Shop when fruits and vegetables are in season.**

The cheapest time to buy fruits and vegetables to supplement your dog's food is when they're in season; you can process and freeze them for later in the year.

Below is a list of some fruits and vegetables for dogs and the best time of year to buy them but, as with any new food, always start off with just a few bites. Some dogs just don't tolerate some foods. Here's a look at each season's best buys:

*Fall*
- Acorn Squash
- Apples (discard seeds)
- Butternut Squash
- Cauliflower
- Figs
- Pears
- Pumpkin
- Sweet Potatoes

*Winter*
- Radishes
- Rutabagas
- Turnips

*Spring*
- Apricots
- Artichoke
- Asparagus
- Carrots
- Mango
- Spinach
- Strawberries

- Snow Peas
- Sugar Snap Peas

*Summer*

- Blackberries
- Blueberries
- Broccoli
- Corn
- Eggplant
- Green Beans
- Peaches
- Plums
- Raspberries
- Watermelon
- Zucchini

**Don't feed your dog cooked bones**.

That stew bone may look and smell tasty but, because it has been cooked, it has become dehydrated and it will splinter easily. Those sharp splinters can result in some painful and very dangerous stomach injuries along with very expensive veterinary care.

**Know which foods *never* to feed your dog.**

Although making your own dog food and treats can be a healthy and economical way to feed your dog, you must know which foods to *never* feed your dog. These foods are toxic to dogs and must always be avoided:

- Apricot pits
- Avocados
- Alcohol

- Apple seeds
- Cherry pits
- Chocolate
- Coffee (and other caffeinated drinks)
- Garlic: some people feed small amounts of garlic but only in moderation.
- Grapes and raisins: because they are condensed, raisins are more dangerous than grapes; avoid cereals and cookies with raisins.
- Macadamia nuts
- Onions
- Peach pits
- Persimmons: the seeds can cause problems
- Plum pits
- Potato peels: discard the peel and any green portions of the potato.
- Tea
- Yeast dough: uncooked dough is very dangerous to your dog.
- Xylitol: used in some diet foods and all diet gums, it is highly toxic to dogs.

**Band together with raw feeders**.

Whether you cook your own dog food or you feed raw, you can band together with raw feeders to buy larger quantities of meat at a better price. Don't know any other raw feeders? Look for Yahoo! Groups in your area, ask Meetup members in your city, etc.

**Buy an electric food grinder.**

If you go the raw food route (or even if you decide to cook your own dog food), a food grinder can be very handy to prepare an appropriate mix of meat and vegetables. Again, check thrift stores, Craigslist and eBay for bargains.

Grinding your own food is much less expensive than buying ground meat or canned dog food and you can cut away the fat to prepare a healthier meal.

**Locate meat processing plants.**

If you prepare your dog's food (either cooked or raw), you can save money by buying directly from meat processing plants in your area.

**Talk with wild game processors.**

During hunting season, wild game processors sometimes sell a mix for dogs; you can also obtain low-cost antlers and bones.

**Visit your butcher.**

Visit a local butcher (not the butcher in your supermarket who may receive meat pre-processed). Ask if he sells low-cost cuts. Let's face it: some cuts of meat just aren't attractive to shoppers but they'll be very attractive to your dog.

**Buy a food dehydrator.**

Buying dehydrated meats and vegetables is convenient—and costly—but you can make them yourself very easily with a food dehydrator.

*Look at thrift stores, on eBay, and on Craigslist for used dehydrators. We snagged one for $5 at a thrift store and it makes great dehydrated sweet potato treats for our dogs!*

special tip

# Shopping at Pet Supply Stores

*Pet supply stores—from mega-stores to mom and pop boutique shops—are great places to get a good selection of dog items. You'll find a variety of ways to save at these stores which work hard to build a loyal customer base.*

### Sign up for loyalty cards.

PetSmart and PETCO both offer loyalty cards to shoppers. It only takes a moment to sign up for these cards and they can save you on purchases at checkout and will also reward you with periodic coupons and discounts based on your past purchases.

### Ask about frequent purchase programs.

Ask your pet supply store if they offer any special programs for dog food purchases. For example, PETCO offers a free food program; for every 10 bags of dog food you purchase (and they must be the same brand and size of premium food purchased within 12 months), you'll earn a coupon for a free bag of that food.

### Use coupons at pet supply stores.

Did you know you can use manufacturer's coupons at most pet supply stores? Just as you'd turn in coupons at the grocery store, most pet supply stores will allow you to use manufacturer's coupons; pair them with store coupons for a real deal!

### Ask pet supply stores for free samples of premium dog foods.

Premium dog foods cost more but the quality you're getting can really tilt the financial scales. Because the food is of higher quality, you don't have to feed your dog as much food at the same meal so the cost can be closer to mass-market kibble than you might think.

Before you pick up that 20-pound sack of premium dog food, though, ask if the store has free samples. Many of the premium dog food manufacturers provide samples to pet supply stores, free for the asking. We've had really good luck at small, independent pet supply stores. Find out which food your dog likes best before you invest in that big sack.

*Dog shows and expos are another good source for free samples and sometimes you'll find free offers on the manufacturer's website, too. (And it never hurts to ask!)*

special tip

## Shopping at Membership Clubs

*If you have friends or coworkers you can split purchases with (or if you have a lot of storage room in your house), membership clubs can be a good shopping option for your pet needs. We have had memberships in the past but we don't now; the nearest one is three times further away than our grocery store.*

**Ask about a trial visit at membership clubs.**

Before buying an annual membership at membership clubs like Sam's Club and Costco, ask about a trial visit. While there, check the availability of your favorite brands of pet supplies and compare the price—per pound—to your regular grocery store and pet supply store. Carry your price book along to compare.

**Weigh the benefits of a membership club.**

Membership clubs are a good fit for some shoppers but not for all. You'll need to weigh the annual cost of your membership against your anticipated savings. Generally you won't find high-end dog foods at membership clubs and you may not always find the same dog foods in stock.

Take advantage of a trial visit (see above) to check out the food selection. If you cook your dog's food, you'll have many more options at the membership club—but you'll usually need to buy in large quantities. Decide if you have storage space and if you'll be able to use or freeze your purchases before they go bad.

Finally, check on store locations since there aren't nearly as many membership clubs as grocery stores. We don't have a membership club card because it's about a 45-minute drive to our nearest one so we'd burn up much of that savings in gas!

**Buy in bulk.**

Buying in bulk at membership clubs can save you money—if you've got the storage capacity. Be sure to take along a calculator to figure a per pound cost and then compare it to what you're usually spending per pound for the same food at the grocery store.

**Share/swap bulk dog food with friends.**

Those jumbo sacks of dog food from the membership clubs are not only difficult to store, but they can also be awfully monotonous for your dog to eat.

The answer: buy several bags of different variety of bulk dog food and divide them with dog-loving family members and friends. It's easier to find a place to store five 10-pound batches of food than one jumbo 50-pound sack, and your dog will enjoy the variety. Be sure one of you saves the sacks, though, in case of a future dog food recall.

Another option, if you have a freezer, is to divide the dry food into zippered bags and freeze them to keep the food fresh.

**Use your warehouse club membership for other pet discounts.**

Membership clubs often offer some discounts on pet-related services. If you have a membership, check the club's website for additional discounts. For example, Sam's Club presently offers a 5 percent discount on the annual premium for Veterinary Pet Insurance (VPI) .

# Feeding & Treating Your Dog

*Whatever you choose to feed your dog—raw or homemade, kibble or canned, the way you feed your dog and store that dog food can impact your bottom line when it comes to your expenditures.*

**Measure your dog's food.**

How much should your dog be eating every day based on his weight and activity level? Do you really know? All too often, it's easy to just pour dry kibble in the bowl but that might not be the appropriate amount.

Replace your food scoop with a measuring cup (yes, we got one of those at the thrift store, too!) Overfeeding not only fattens your dog and wastes food but it also can potentially lead to costly veterinary bills.

Also, realize that the daily potions on the dog food bag are usually for an active, unaltered dog; your dog's needs may be lower.

*An excellent way to know if your dog is overweight is to feel his ribs; they should feel similar to the back of your hand and be slightly visible. Your dog should also have an indentation for his "waist" when viewed from above.*

**Reward your dog with fun.**

Treats are just one way to reward and praise your dog. A completely free way to reward your dog—with play and praise—is good for your pocketbook and both your waistlines!

**Encourage your dog to like a food.**

Have you ever bought a dog food your dog didn't really care for? We recently purchased a $15 bag of premium food for our dogs. Our Irie loved it—and our dog Tiki turned up her nose at it. We could have kept the bag for Irie but we decided to try a little "reflavoring" and see if it might make the food more appealing to Tiki.

We dropped a few of her favorite, strongly-flavored treats in the sack of dog food and tightly sealed it for a couple of days. When we gave the food another try, Tiki absolutely loved the food—which by then had absorbed the scent of her favorite treats!

**Store your dog's food carefully.**

Especially when you buy dog food in bulk, it's important to properly store the food or it will go bad and have to be thrown out…throwing out your saving as well. You'll find specially made pet food storage bins but one of the best ways to store food for more than a couple of weeks is by freezing it.

You can opt for zippered freezer bags or invest in a vacuum food sealing system (we've seen them at thrift stores!) By freezing the food, you'll lock in the flavor; stale food has less aroma so your dog is less likely to eat it. (If you feed probiotics foods, check with the manufacturer for any impact freezing might have on the active cultures used in the food.)

**Make your own dog treats.**

Even if you're not ready to commit to making your dog's food, you can save by preparing treats at home for your dog. Treats are inexpensive and simple to make. Here's a recipe for Peanut Butter Bones, one of our dogs' favorites!

- 1 cup peanut butter
- 1 cup whole wheat flour
- 1 cup all-purpose flour
- 2 tablespoons olive oil
- 1 cup multigrain cereal or bran flakes, crushed (do NOT use cereals with raisins)
- 1/2 cup shredded carrots
- 2 tablespoons baking powder
- 1 tablespoon molasses
- 1/2 cup water

Mix the dry ingredients then add the wet ingredients, adding the water a little at a time. The amount of water you'll need will vary based on the moisture in the peanut butter. Work the dough on a lightly floured surface (if the dough's too sticky, sprinkle with more flour…if it's too dry, add just a little water.)

Roll out the dough to about a 1/4-inch thickness then it's time to cut with a cookie cutter. Place on a greased cookie sheet, bake at 350 degrees for about 25 minutes until both sides are lightly browned, then cool treats before refrigerating.

**Make your dog a cool, cheap treat: ice!**

Our dogs love ice cubes on a hot day—and what a treat for our budget! To make it a real treat, add bits of fruit, vegetables or bits of hot dogs or chicken to the water and freeze it in a small plastic tub or ice cube trays. Add a bit of beef or chicken broth to add flavor, nutrition and fun for your dog for just pennies per treat!

**Make your own liver training treats.**

One of the easiest and most popular dog treats we've found is liver. Liver makes a nutritious snack that dogs absolutely love. We cut it into small pieces and use it as training treats; it's a strong motivator!

To make liver training treats, preheat your oven to 325 degrees. Place a single layer of thawed liver on a lightly greased cookie sheet. Bake for 30 minutes. When done, allow the liver to cool then cut into treats the size of coins and refrigerate. That's it...an easy, inexpensive treat that's sure to fetch some real attention!

# Dog Toys

One of the reasons we love dogs is the joy we feel when seeing them happily playing, whether with us, with each other, or just having a ball all by themselves. When expressing themselves through play, our dogs are telling us that they are happy and healthy and are also displaying quite a bit of their true personalities. Just as children learn and develop through play, our pets need the stimulation, both mental and physical, that play can provide to develop their full potential.

Left to their own devices, most dogs will find toys to play with but in some cases these might not be considered "toys" to us (like your shoes, for example, or the chewy garden hose). Instead, offer them a variety of well-chosen toys to spark their interest.

# Buying Bargains

*Unlike children, dogs don't ask for the season's hottest toy; they're perfectly happy with toys you find on sale, used toys, and repurposed materials that have been transformed into toys!*

**Buy children's toys.**

> Many toys designed for young children also make good dog toys and are often cheaper to purchase. Many more human toys than dog toys can be found at thrift shops and garage sales.

> Most toys designed for children should be safe for puppies and dogs but it's always best to examine each toy closely and note any possible hazards. We like buying infant and toddler toys since they're made with the assumption that they'll be chewed.

> Remove any hard pieces such as metal or plastic eyes from stuffed toys, and skip soft plastic toys that might be too easy for a dog to chew up and swallow.

**Clean used toys.**

> It's important to clean used dog toys before giving them to your dog. Plush toys can be laundered and then thoroughly dried on cotton setting to kill germs. Toys with hard surfaces should be cleaned with a properly diluted bleach solution to kill germs then thoroughly rinsed and dried.

**Buy holiday toys off season.**

> Squeaky Santas will be equally loved in April or August. Last November we bought squeaky Halloween pumpkin toys at 90 percent off and when we gave them to the dogs in February, the dogs loved them!

**Shop thrift stores and garage sales.**

Stuffed dog toys have a pretty short lifespan around our house. Check out your local thrift store for stuffed animals. You'll find a huge assortment at most stores and prices that start as low as 25 cents. Garage sales are another good option.

In either case, make sure the toys have no hard parts (especially eyes) that your dog could chew off. Also, watch for microbeads in stuffed toys and pass over those that feel like they're weighted with small plastic pellets.

**Buy good quality chew toys.**

Our Lab mix can go through cheap chew toys in a matter of hours (if that long). If you have a power chewer in your house, it's more economical to invest in high quality dog toys such as Kong, a firm rubber toy/treat dispenser that comes in classic and extreme levels of durability, than to buy numerous cheap dog chew toys that your dog can go through like dog biscuits!

Around these power chewers, cheap chew toys aren't just messy, they're dangerous as you run the risk of your dog choking on or ingesting part of the toy.

# Get Creative

*Toys don't have to be purchased in the dog toy aisle to provide a lot of fun and mental stimulation for your dog. One important tip to remember: don't repurpose anything into a toy that you wouldn't want chewed or destroyed in everyday life. For example, don't ever turn an old sneaker into a toy; your dog has no way to know the difference in what you consider an old shoe and a good shoe!*

**Make a toy from a water bottle.**

Kari Whitman, a special correspondent for "Extra" television show and also a dog savior—her nonprofit Ace of Hearts saves shelter dogs on the day they are scheduled to be euthanized, sent us a special money-saving tip for toys.

"Take a colorful old sock that's lost its mate and slip a small (empty!) plastic water bottle inside. Tie a knot at the top of the sock and you have the perfect toy to play fetch! Not too noisy, not too heavy and it won't damage any precious heirlooms if it hits something! Best of all it will keep your pup happy and occupied for hours. (Please note that if your pup loves to chew everything in sight, plastic water bottles may be harmful if ingested.)"

celebrity tip

**Make a pull toy from braided t-shirts.**

We don't know about you, but somehow, our closets always seem to be full of t-shirts, many of which we seldom wear. Well, it's easy to turn some of those t-shirts into a tough dog toy.

Just gather up three shirts and cut each one into a long 2-inch-wide strip by starting your cut from the bottom of the shirt and spiraling upward to the top of the shirt.

Tie a knot with all three strands at one end of the strands. Anchor the knot against the wall or a piece of furniture (we have a nail in just the right place on a front porch column) then proceed to braid the three strands into a flat braid. As you reach the end of the strands, tie another knot.

*Voila*, your dog has a new toy for playing tug-of-war. He will love it because you made it for him and maybe because it smells like you!

**Use paper plate holders as Frisbees.**

For some reason, paper plate holders are always available at thrift stores, often sold by batch for as little as $1 a dozen. They make fun Frisbees (although they won't sail as far).

**Make a treat dispenser from an old football.**

Do you have an old football (or other firm but inflatable ball) around the house? We had a miniature football...not the hard plastic kind but one of the inflatable ones. We'd purchased it for the dogs at a thrift store...and they showed zero interest in it.

Using a sharp pocketknife, John cut two, nickel-sized holes in the football. (The first one is easiest to cut; once the air's out of the football, it gets a little trickier. Be careful!)

special tip

*NOTE: It's very important to cut at least two holes in the football, not just one! Your dog's tongue can be suctioned to the toy and injured if you just cut one hole. As with any dog toy, always supervise your dog when playing then pick it up when play is over.*

When you cut the piece out of the football, check the inside of the ball (just look at the back of the piece) and make sure the football interior looks clean. After you've cut out two or more pieces, drop in a handful of kibble and treats and stand back and watch the fun!

**Make your own dog toys.**

Get innovative with items you have around the house and create your own dog toys! Cut jeans into strips and tie them together for a tug of war rope. Drill holes through a tennis ball (or use a plastic whiffle ball) then thread blue jean strips through the holes; finally, tie knots on each end for a fun toy to toss.

**Use a child's sandbox for dogs.**

Visit a thrift store and you just might come across a plastic child's sandbox (these seem to get donated a lot...maybe it's their large size.) Made of heavy-duty plastic, the sand box has two great uses for dogs:

- **a swimming pool.** This shallow pool is a great splash and play pool (and won't try to bend in half like thinner children's wading pools when you tip it over to dump out the water.)

- **a dog's sand box.** Do you have a dog that loves to dig? Redirect him! Fill the sandbox with sand, soil or a mixture and bury some bones, biscuits, or treats inside...then turn your dog loose and let him fulfill his natural instincts to dig. These sand boxes often come with a lid so you can cover the box at night (and prevent your sand box from becoming a litter box for neighborhood cats).

**Buy replacement squeakers.**

Many dogs love toys with an embedded squeaker, usually a small plastic bladder which emits a squeak when chewed or mashed with a paw. Our dog Tiki, for example, noses through the doggie toy box to find her favorite toys that squeak when she plays with them. However, those little bladders are prone to punctures.

Replacement squeakers are cheap (under $1) and can be found at many dog supply stores, online, or at dog shows.

All you need to do is remove the old bladder, insert the new one and sew the toy closed. (We also buy replacement squeakers to add to homemade dog toys.) Double the fun and toss in a couple of squeakers at opposite ends of the toy!

special tip

*NOTE: If you have a real power chewer, never leave your dog alone with a squeaky toy because of the danger of tearing into the toy and choking on that squeaker. Our Irie rips into toys so the squeaking toys are handed out to her only when she's playing near us.*

**Remove stuffing.**

Our lab mix loves stuffed animals…she loves them so much the house, the yard, and everything in-between are soon covered in toy stuffing. You'll find non-stuffed toys at pet stores but it's cheaper to make your own. (Dogs have a practical reason for unstuffing their toys; females need to be able to teach puppies the skill of ripping fur and pulling off meat.)

While occasionally you might not mind picking up after this practice session, at other times you might want to give your dog a toy and not have to plan for a cleanup time later—and you never want your dog to potentially ingest that stuffing which can cause intestinal blockage (and even worse if the toy has fire retardant stuffing.)

The answer? Unstuff your toys. We scour local thrift stores for inexpensive used toys (anywhere from 25 cents to $1).

First, cut out all plastic parts such as eyes and the nose. These can cause real problems if your dog pulls them out and swallows or chews them (most have sharp backs). Using the opening you've creating when cutting out the eyes and nose, start reaching in and

61

pulling out the stuffing. Turn the arms and legs inside out and grab all the stuffing. Pay special attention to make sure the toy doesn't have micro plastic beads (they're used to weigh dolls so they'll "sit up." Toss them all.)

When you've pulled out all the stuffing, you can insert a squeaker inside the toy if you like. Finally, sew up the opening you cut to remove the eyes then the stuffing. No need for anything fancy, just some quick stitches…and you're done! Your dog has a new toy, you've got a pile of stuffing you can use for another project, and you've saved yourself a big pickup job!

**Rotate those toys.**

Just like children, dogs tire of the same toys so don't leave them with their toys for an extended period of time. By rotating out the toys, you'll be giving him a "new" toy without having to actually buy a new toy!

# Training and Exercise

Dog training is a vital part of your dog's life. Poorly trained dogs can create havoc in a home, develop habits ranging from annoying nipping to dangerous aggression, and get into (costly) accidents or become lost because they won't come when called.

Too many owners don't take the time to train their dogs—then wonder why their dog won't behave properly! The result: all too many dogs wind up in shelters.

One aspect of training that's important to realize is that, aside from the socialization a dog receives around other dogs and humans in a class, much of the training in a class is the training of you. An hour-long class once a week, taken with your dog, will give you the skills you need to train your dog but it doesn't provide enough in-class time to actually train your dog. That's something that you and your dog will work on—

on a daily basis—for his entire life. It's a bonding experience and one that should be fun for both you and your dog.

(You will find boarding training programs where you drop your dog off and pick him up—supposedly trained—weeks later. You won't learn how to train him, you won't be bonding with your dog, and your dog will learn to see someone else as leader—and you'll spend a ton of money. Skip this option.)

## Saving on Professional Dog Training

*Classes taught by professional dog trainers can pay for themselves time and time again. To find a professional dog trainer in your area, check the Association of Pet Dog Trainers website, www.apdt.com.*

**Realize that classes are cheaper than replacement furniture.**

> To be honest, a comprehensive inventory of dog-related expenses should include wear and tear on the family domicile. While not a direct cost, there's no doubt that dogs, especially untrained ones, can add to the costs of upkeep. From that perspective, enrolling Fido in a behavior class can be a good investment, in addition to the numerous other benefits of having a well-trained, well-behaved pet.

> A basic short (group) course generally starts at as little as $100. After basic training, the only cost to you will be the time you spend helping your dog become a good dog citizen.

**Ask about buddy discounts.**

> Some dog training companies offer "buddy discounts" for you and a friend and your dogs. Not only will the two of you save money, but you'll have a buddy for practicing those new skills!

**Ask your vet clinic if they refer clients to dog trainers.**

Some dog trainers offer referral programs to veterinary offices, giving clients a discount.

**Ask if you can observe a training session.**

Before signing up for dog training classes, ask if you can sit in and observe a training session. You'll get a better idea of the trainer's style and if he or she is a good match for you and your dog—*before* you pay for those lessons.

**Ask your shelter if they offer training classes.**

Some shelters offer training classes, sometimes at a discount if you have recently adopted a dog. We've also seen shelters that will offer training for a few dogs that have been harder to place.

**Ask your shelter if they've partnered with any dog trainers.**

With each adoption, some shelters offer discounted training with dog training companies they've partnered with; when you adopt, ask if they work with any dog trainers in the area.

**Look for group classes instead of individual classes.**

Look for about a 50 percent savings on group classes rather than individual classes. Group classes will also allow your dog to socialize with other dogs and people, an important skill.

**Sign up for an informal puppy class.**

Designed for puppies from 3 to 6 months old, puppy classes usually concentrate on ensuring that your puppy grows into well-socialized dog. This will enable your puppy to behave appropriately around other dogs and around people.

In addition to encouraging socialization, puppies can be introduced to basic skills such as coming when called, and walking on a leash.

Prices for puppy classes usually start around $50. By starting puppies out on the right paw, early training can prevent problem behaviors when he matures.

### Join a training club.

Ask other dog lovers if there's a dog training club in your area. For example, Michigan's Kalamazoo Training Club, (*www.kdtc.org*) offers seven weeks of training classes starting at just $60 and reduced fees for dogs recently adopted from animal control or area rescues.

### Barter your skills for dog services.

Do you need a dog trainer? A groomer? A dog sitter? You might be able to barter your own skills.

First, decide what skills you have to barter with—whether it's dog-related skills (walking, grooming, pet sitting) or non-related (tax preparation, housecleaning, baking). *Craigslist.org* has extensive barter boards arranged by state, a good starting point.

Also, sites like *www.TimeBanks.org* help you barter by "banking" your time in exchange for someone else's time; the site lists time banks worldwide.

# DIY Dog Training

*Much of the work involved in dog training is actually training you to learn how to train your dog so, if you work at it, you can learn the same skills from videos, online, and books.*

**Check out books on dog training.**

Head to your local library for a free dog training tool: library books. Look for newer training books that teach positive reinforcement so the training will be fun for you and your dog!

**Walk with an older dog.**

Recently we interviewed National Geographic Channel's "Dog Whisperer" Cesar Millan and he provided us with a great tip on teaching your dog without spending a penny—by walking with your neighbor and a balanced, older dog.

celebrity tip

"Get to know your neighbors and get to see which dogs in your neighborhood are balanced. It's an older dog who teaches the puppy the manners of a dog," said Millan. "It's important that we join that person with that dog in the walks. Puppies, they walk, they explore and then they stop and they say 'How do I react to this?' When they are in front of an older dog, the older dog says, '*This* is how we respond to this.'"

**Watch YouTube training videos.**

You'll find numerous dog training videos online that address one specific behavior per video: teaching your dog to stop jumping on people, teaching your dog to come when called, etc. Expert Village has many excellent training videos on YouTube or search for "positive dog training" or "positive reinforcement dog training."

**Ask your shelter about training materials.**

When we adopted Tiki, the shelter offered free printed training materials with our adoption packet and a discounted video on training. Ask your local shelter (even if you didn't adopt from them), if they have any materials on training.

# Dog Supplies and Accessories

Dog supplies range from must-have items like collars and leashes to optional goodies like clothes and jewelry (yes, we said jewelry). If you're craftsy, you'll find many DIY projects from dog sweaters to dog beds.

Even without any knitting or sewing skills, we've found that we've been able to make many of our dog supplies using scissors and very simple stitching and using repurposed items.

Some of these money-saving ideas are just common sense while others are the result of years of trial and error as we've cared for numerous pets. With a little ingenuity, you can cut corners without sacrificing top-notch care for your dog.

# Where to Shop for Dog Supplies

When you think of shopping for your dog's needs, a few prime destinations come to mind: your local grocery store, superstores, pet supply stores, and online pet retailers.

But there are numerous other places to shop for your dog. Here are 10 non-traditional place to shop for your dog's needs:

- **Membership Clubs.** Large membership clubs like Sam's Club and Costco can spell savings but do your research before investing in that membership to see if the store is a good fit for your household.

- **Drugstores.** Dog food, toys, treats, shampoos and more are found at drugstores, and the most competitive chains run frequent specials and offer discount programs.

- **Garage sales.** It takes time and patience (and some gas money) but you can find good deals at garage sales. You'll find everything from bowls to old towels and bedding for your dog, usually at bargain basement prices. At many garage sales, you can snag an extra good deal late in the day and it never hurts to ask if a lower price will be accepted.

- **Thrift stores.** We love thrift stores for their good prices and the ease of shopping (much easier than running from garage sale to garage sale). We buy stainless steel bowls, bedding, toys and much more at our local thrift stores.

- **Livestock feed stores.** Feed stores, found in small communities to serve area farmers and ranchers, sell dog food, bedding (including items like cedar shavings, great for low-cost outdoor bedding that discourages fleas). Similarly, farm and ranch stores don't sell feed but do sell many dog supplies, dog food, fencing materials, and more.

- **Hardware stores.** You'll find dog supplies such as collars and leashes at some hardware stores; look for dog bedding and fencing materials as well.

- **Craigslist.org, Freecycle.org, and eBay.com.** Don't purchase pet medications on these sites but non-medicinal, non-edible purchases can be good bargains. Look for crates, kennels, dog stairs and ramps, and other large items that can easily be cleaned.

- **Pet consignment stores.** A growing number of pet consignment stores are popping up selling "gently used" dog toys, beds, clothes, crates, and more. We haven't found prices at these stores to be as low as comparable buys at garage sales and thrift stores but the advantage is you'll have a good selection of quality items.

- **Dollar stores.** Cleaning supplies are usually good buys at dollar stores. You'll often find dog toys, some food and treats (be sure to check the "best by" dates), stainless steel bowls, and other supplies here, too.

- **Animal shelters.** Many larger shelters operate stores selling everything from flea prevention to dog toys, with proceeds benefiting the shelter.

# Dog Clothes and Accessories

*From clothes to collars, accessories run the gamut when it comes to prices. With some careful shopping, you can purchase or make many items for your dog without breaking your budget.*

**Look for dog consignment stores.**

> Does your city have a dog consignment store? A growing number do (and some traditional consignment stores are offering a selection of high-end dog clothes at a fraction of the price.) You can also find gently used dog bedding and other goodies at these shops. (And when you tire of some of those dog sweaters, you can clean and resell yours at these shops, too!)

**Make a dog sweater from your sweater.**

> Tiki is a 55-pound dog so we started with a women's sweater (medium), selecting a sweater made from a fleecy material that wouldn't unravel when cut (which will happen with a knitted sweater). An old sweatshirt would be another good option.

> This sweater had a cowl neck; if you choose one with a turtleneck, you might have to remove the turtleneck so your dog's head will fit through the neck easily. After removing the sleeves about two inches below the shoulder, cut off the lower front of the sweater a couple of inches below the sleeve level, leaving the back untouched.

> The chest was a little too large so we stitched a seam by hand to tighten up the sweater a little, snipping a half-inch slit in the back, just below the collar, to hook the leash. The result? A stylish sweater that (surprise!) Tiki seemed to enjoy wearing.

**Make a collar cover.**

Does your dog's collar disappear beneath a cloud of dog hair?
We had that problem. Our medium-haired dog, Tiki, always
wears a collar...but you'd never know it just to glance at her. We
tried brightly colored collars but they still worked their way
under the hair on the ruff of her neck. Next, we tried a bright
bandana, tied around her neck as a supplement to the collar. It
looked cute...and it lasted about 15 minutes, thanks to the "help"
she received from our dog Irie.

The solution? A red bandana, cut in half and sewn *around* the
collar. First, cut the bandana in half (not diagonally to produce
pointed ends but through the middle to create two rectangular
pieces.) Set the second piece aside for a future collar.

Next, fold the bandana in half lengthwise. Lay the collar over the
bandana and continue folding the bandana so you create a tube of
bandana around the collar. By hand, sew up the edge. (If you'd
like to be able to wash the bandana, make the tube loose-fitting
around the collar. If your dog is tough on collars, sew it firmly
around the collar so it can't be ripped off.)

Don't worry about pretty stitches but make sure your stitches are
tight, especially on the ends. Your finished product is a bandana-
wrapped collar. You'll still have access to the ends and the tag.
Make sure you loosen the collar a little; the additional fabric will
mean the pre-fitted collar will now be a little tighter on your dog.

**Turn a child's belt into a dog collar.**

Just as if you were sizing a traditional dog collar, measure your
dog's neck, add a few inches, then trim the belt so you won't
have a tempting length leftover to serve as a potential toy. Since
this trim left us short of the belt's holes, we had to punch a new

hole in the heavy vinyl with an ice pick (a leather punch would be ideal, if you have one). Whether you're raiding your closet or hitting the thrift stores, keep these factors in mind when selecting a belt to become a dog collar:

- avoid belts with large buckles

- avoid belts with insets and studs that a second dog could potentially pull off and choke on

- avoid braided belts; they'll unravel when trimmed to size

- select a belt the same width as you would select for a dog collar

- leather belts can be excellent if your dog chews through nylon collars (although some dogs will *really* like the leather) but they can shrink and get stiff if your dog is a swimmer

- look for belts with a simple loop to tuck under the extra length; you can also use this loop to hang a dog tag (use a keychain loop if you need something larger than the traditional dog tag loop)

- don't select belts with an end narrower than the belt itself or you'll need to recut the end to fit through the buckle once you trim the belt for length

**Make your own personalized dog collar.**

For a budget solution, purchase a light color (solid color) woven nylon dog collar. With a permanent marker such as a Sharpie, write in large letters your last name and full phone number with area code.

# Looking for Sales

*Whether it's a dog bed or bowl, all dog supplies go on sale some time or another, some place or another. Saving money is just a matter of planning ahead so you can look for the sales rather than waiting until you need the item right away.*

**Know when dog-related items go on sale.**

Sales on larger purchases follow an annual calendar, a time when you can save money on new purchases of these items (and have better luck finding used ones at thrift stores as people replace their goods!)

- January: Carpet and flooring; linens; towels; rugs
- April and May: vacuum cleaners
- August: linens; towels

**Buy supplies off season.**

Buy plush dog beds, dog sweaters, etc. at the end of winter season. Like to dress up for Halloween? Hit the sales right after the event and you'll be set for next year. If you enjoy dressing up your dog for Halloween, early November is the time to stock up for next year. Similarly you'll find summer merchandise—from life vests to cooling beds—marked down at the end of the season.

After-Christmas sales are a great time to stock up on dog goodies, often at prices up to 75 percent off. Before New Year's, check pet supply stores for good discounts on:

- **holiday treats and chews.** Your dog won't care one bit if the treat is shaped like a candy cane—and the treat for you is the savings.

- **holiday collars.** Besides jingle bell collars, you'll find some practical collars on sale many places. And if they sport Santas and snowflakes, so be it!

- **holiday sweaters.** Buy dog sweaters at the end of the year and your pooch will still have months of chilly days to wear those holiday sweaters (and dogs will not laugh at other dogs at the dog park if they're sporting elf sweaters in February.)

- **dog calendars.** Like other calendars, dog calendars go on sale by New Year's Day; by the first and second week of January, you'll find huge discounts.

## Shopping Online for Dog Supplies

*The number of online stores selling dog items continues to grow; that healthy competition can mean good sales, if you look. You can extend your savings by looking for free shipping offers as well.*

**Search price aggregators.**

Sites like *www.pricegrabber.com* will do your comparison shopping for you to help you find the best bargains. A quick search of this site found over 15,000 dog bed listings, nearly 400 listings for dog bones, and plenty of other pet goodies. Other popular deal aggregators include *www.dealslist.com* and *dealnews.com*.

**Search for online store coupons.**

Check for online coupons before placing your online order by doing a quick search like "roomba coupons" or "roomba coupon code" before you do your ordering. We recently ordered a

Roomba automatic vacuum and found a $25 coupon and a free shipping code for it this way!

**Sign up for rebate programs.**

Several online rebate programs offer you a percentage discount for each purchase and many of these programs feature numerous pet supply stores.

For example, *MrRebates.com* presently offers over 2,000 cash back online stores including PETCO, 1800PetMeds.com, Dog.com, and more. The day we checked, rebates range up to 12 percent. Similarly, *www.Ebates.com* offers over 1,200 online shops (pet-related shops are located under the "Home and Garden" category). You'll find coupons as well as cash back refunds.

**Find free shipping.**

Numerous online retailers offer free shipping, sometimes tied to the amount of purchase. Some sites, like Amazon, clearly state their free shipping policy right on the site but at others you'll need a free shipping coupon code. To find these free shipping coupon codes, check sites like *www.freeshipping.org*, *www.retailmenot.com*, and *www.myretailcodes.com*.

Another strategy: search for the name of the online store and the phrase "free shipping" to fetch those codes!

**Join a Freecycle group.**

With over seven million members around the globe, Freecycle (*www.freecycle.org*) groups offer free give and take opportunities to keep items out of landfills—and this includes useful items for dog families. You'll join a group in your area, search for items you need for your dog such as dog houses, fencing, or bedding—and don't forget to give back with some items you can no longer use but someone else might!

**Ask if returns can be made to the store.**

Although you might make your purchase online, if you need to return an item you just might be able to make the return at the store, saving on shipping fees. Walmart.com, Target.com, and others allow you to return items directly to brick and mortar stores.

# Do-It-Yourself Dog Supplies

*You don't have to be a seamstress, a woodworker, or a crafter to make some simple, do-it-yourself dog supplies. Often you'll find a repurposing of other materials or a simple hand-sewn seam can transform what had been discarded items into a useful (and free) product for your dog!*

**Make an ant-resistant bowl.**

You can purchase special bowls to keep ants out of your dog's food or you can make your own very easily. Find a tray with a slight lip and nearly fill the tray with water. Place your dog's bowl in the middle of the tray; the ants won't be able to cross the water to the food.

**Make a chew-proof dog bed from jeans.**

We've purchased cheap beds and expensive "chew proof" beds and, when our dogs were adolescent puppies, Irie and Tiki managed to tear their way into the beds every time. The solution: a heavy-duty dog bed made from heavy blue jeans. This inexpensive project takes an hour or two of time. You'll need:

- one or two pairs of jeans (depending on the size of the dog and the size of your jeans)

- needle and thread (a sewing machine is great but this can be done by hand)

- cedar bedding (about $7 a bundle at garden supply stores or feed stores. A bundle is enough to fill two or three large dog beds)

First, select the heaviest jeans you've got in the rag box. Don't use jeans with torn knees or pockets or those with thin material. If you have a small dog, opt for children's jeans or just the leg of a pair of jeans. If your dog's large and your pants aren't, head to the thrift store for inexpensive jeans in an array of sizes.

Turn the jeans inside out. Hem the jeans straight across about one inch from the bottom so that when you turn the pants right side out, the bottom seam will be inside the legs (and harder for your dog to tear apart).

Next, tack the two legs together at least four places down the inside seam to form a solid pillow. Sew the zipper fly shut.

Take your cedar bedding and fill the jeans from the waist. Holding the pants up, fill the pants about 2/3rds full so there's still a little room for your dog to push the pillow down and get cozy in it. If you don't have any cedar bedding, you can use rags, old pillows, etc. as your bedding.

Sew the waist shut. If you're sewing by hand, sew just beneath the waistband (you won't be able to get a needle through the heavy waistband by hand). You can use non-toxic liquid fabric glue, available in fabric stores, to glue the waistband shut after you sew it.

Lastly, top the bed with any fleecy or fake sheepskin material you might have to make it extra cozy (but know that this will be the weak point in the bed since it will be the easiest to rip off).

**Make a large dog bed from a child's sleeping bag.**

Once our dogs stopped ripping through beds like they were made of paper towels, we were able to make softer beds for them. One of our dogs' favorites beds began life as a child's sleeping bag. Made of plush material, the sleeping bag was easily stuffed with clothes that were ready for the rag bag.

We stitched up the top of the bag, sewed the zipper pull inside the bag so it was out of reach, and the sleeping bag was suddenly a great dog bed!

**Recycle bags to use as poop bags.**

Kari Whitman, who works as a special correspondent for television's "Extra" and runs an amazing non-profit to save shelter dogs called Ace of Hearts, gave us a great tip on saving money on dog waste bags:

celebrity tip

"Save money and the environment by crossing poop bags off your shopping list. Instead of buying new bags, recycle plastic bags from the grocery store, plastic newspaper sleeves, or newspapers themselves to pick up after your pooch. It's 100 percent free and 100 percent as effective!"

**Make a dog bed from a zippered pillowcase.**

For smaller dogs, zippered pillowcases can make excellent dog beds. Fill the pillowcases with rags and zip shut; when it's time for a wash, it's easy to unstuff and wash the pillow and its contents before drying and restuffing.

**Make a dog rag bag.**

>   Rather than buying paper towels to clean dog messes, make a rag
>   box of old towels, jeans, and t-shirts. Cut them to a convenient
>   size (that way when they go through the wash, you won't
>   mistakenly put them back in the closet.)

**Slow your dog's eating.**

>   Does your dog gulp his food? Our lab mix Irie does and, with
>   such a deep-chested dog, it is a habit that can cause some serious
>   problems, namely Bloat (or formally, Gastric Dilatation Volvulus
>   or GDV). You'll find dog bowls designed to slow eating by
>   means of obstructions in the bowl, segments, and spreading the
>   food out over a wider area (instead of in a pile your dog can just
>   vacuum up in a bite or two).
>
>   Looking for a recycled solution? Try a muffin tin. We bought one
>   at a thrift store for $1 and it works as well as the $30+ specialty
>   bowls for slowing Irie's eating.
>
>   The multiple cups make your dog slow down during mealtime.
>   Each regular size muffin holder can hold about 3.5 ounces; a
>   jumbo muffin or cupcake holder will hold about eight ounces.
>   Avoid ones with Teflon coating since your dog may chip the
>   coating with his teeth.
>
>   Another option: invert a bowl in a larger bowl (or on a large
>   plate) so your dog has to eat around the smaller, upside-down
>   bowl. It will slow his eating down!

# Repurposing Used Items for Your Dog

*Sometimes when shopping for used items, you have to keep an open
mind. Could that sleeping bag make a good dog bed? Would the*

*stainless steel mixing bowl work as a dog water bowl? Repurposing items you find at thrift stores and garage sales can help you meet many of your dog supply needs at a very low cost!*

**Shop at thrift stores.**

> We love shopping thrift stores for items for ourselves, our pets, and our home. Offering donated and usually (but not always) used merchandise, thrift stores feature all types of items with price tags at just a fraction of the original price.
>
> The inventory at these stores varies from day to day so it often pays to shop a few times and to be open-minded and flexible (you might not find a giant blue pillow like you want to use as a dog bed...but you might find a nice red one).
>
> You'll find dog supplies on occasion and you'll always find merchandise that can be repurposed with some creative thinking. Here's a sampling of some of the types of items we've found for our dogs at thrift stores:
>
> - **Stainless steel bowls.** We use these for our dogs' water and food. The bowls will often be mixing bowls or salad bowls and stocked with the household goods.
>
> - **Large floor pillows.** These make excellent dog beds.
>
> - **Used towels.** We've used these for everything from bedding to dog baths.
>
> - **Comforters, bedspreads and quilts.** We've used these for dog bedding as well as for slipcovers for our couch. We always keep a blanket over our couch; it's just a fraction of the cost of slipcovers.

- **Children's toys.** We modify children's toys as dog toys (see the "Dog Toy" section for more detail.)

- **Heavy jeans.** We've transformed these into chew-proof dog beds.

- **Children's belts.** We turned these into dog collars during our dogs' chewing phase when they chewed collars off of one another faster than we could buy them.

- **Muffin tins**. We've served our fast-eating dog out of muffin tins to slow her eating.

- **Food dehydrator.** We bought one for $5 to dry jerky or vegetables (perfect for taking advantage of seasonal specials).

**Look for sales days at thrift stores.**

Like any other store, most thrift stores have sales, too. At our local thrift store, for example, a certain color price tag goes on sale each week. (They tag merchandise by arrival date so this moves stuff that's been sitting around the store for a while.)

We save 50 percent on already low prices when they're on sale—which sometimes tips the scales in deciding whether to buy and repair a torn comforter to use as a couch cover.

**Use children's steps for small to medium-sized dogs.**

Children's steps, the two- and three-step items made to use to reach the sink or help parents in the kitchen, can be great for older dogs that need a little help getting up on the bed, their favorite chair, or the couch. You'll usually be able to find these at thrift stores or at children's consignment stores.

**Buy a baby gate as dog gate.**

Need to restrict a new dog from certain rooms of your house? Pet superstores sell special dog gates to prevent access – but look for baby gates at thrift stores and garage sales at a fraction of the price. We have a two-story house and the upstairs contains our home offices—and all the computer cords and electrical wires that go along with that. When we first got our dogs, we purchased a baby gate for $3 to prevent them from going upstairs.

# Grooming and Other Services

Taking your dog to the groomer for haircuts, baths, and nail trims adds up and, unlike veterinary care, grooming is a skill that you can learn. After all, this is one skill that doesn't have to be perfect to be efficient, and we promise your dog won't complain one bit if his haircut's a little uneven.

Grooming your dog at home can be fun (yes, really!), it can be a bonding experience for you and your dog, and it can definitely help your pocketbook.

The same goes for many other dog services such as dog walking and boarding. Whether you opt to do them yourself or to rely on the help of neighbors and friends, trimming these items from your budget can add up quickly.

# At the Groomer

*If you don't want to give up professional grooming, you'll still find that there are ways to cut your costs. Sometimes all it requires is for you to ask about specials and discounts.*

**Cut back on grooming frequency.**

> Can't stand to go the do-it-yourself route when it comes to grooming? Then make your groomer visits less frequent. Space out those visits by allowing another two or three weeks between hair cuts.
>
> One way to do this is to ask your groomer to cut your dog's hair a "step" shorter. Like having your own hair trimmed shorter, this will extend the life of your dog's haircut—and extend the savings.
>
> Others save money by having their dog shaved during the summer months (not recommended for dogs with a lot of sun exposure, though, since his fur is protecting him from sunburn).

**Ask about referral programs.**

> Ask your groomer if he offers a referral program so you can earn discounts or free grooming sessions for referring new clients.

**Don't waste money on teeth brushing at the groomer.**

> Groomers charge $10 to $20 to brush your dog's teeth. Brushing your dog's teeth is great—but you need to do it far more often than the six- or eight-week visit to the groomer. Save your money and brush your dog's teeth at home every few days.

**Ask for nail trimming tips.**

Whether you get your dog's nails trimmed at the vet's office or at the groomer, ask if you can watch and learn. Also, check video sites like YouTube for how-to videos. It's not difficult to do with most dogs (especially if your dog has white nails that allow you to see the pink vein inside the nail. It's more difficult with black nails.)

We trim our dog Irie's nails every week because the quick grows close to the end of the nail and we can't trim off much each session. (Think what we save in nail trimming fees.) We got her accustomed to having her feet handled by massaging her feet when we're just sitting around watching TV. When we started trimming, we trimmed just a nail or two at first, accompanied by lots of treats and praise.

Our dog Tiki doesn't need such frequent trims. Some of her nails are white and some are black. We trim the white ones first then clip the same amount off the black nails to avoid a painful cut.

**Avoid dematting fees.**

Even if you'll still be taking your dog to the groomer, avoid dematting fees by brushing out your dog's hair every day or two. Make a habit of removing burrs and detangling hair after every walk then sit down for a full brushing every day or two.

Often burrs removes easily if you get it out right away. If you find an especially stubborn burr, try crushing it with pliers then picking out the pieces from your dog's hair.

You'll save as much as 30 percent on your next grooming bill by dematting your dog yourself.

**Look for a dog grooming school.**

> Is there a dog grooming school in your area? You can often book discounted grooming services at many dog grooming schools.

**Avoid flea killing fees.**

> Groomers will use a flea killing shampoo or, sometimes, instant flea killing medication if a dog comes in with fleas. Avoid these charges of about $10 by making sure your dog is flea-free when he arrives at the groomer.

**Ask if there's a "frequent groom" program.**

> If you regularly take you dog to the groomer, ask if they have a program to earn a free groom. For example, at PETCO after you buy eight full-service grooms, full-service baths or self-service dog washes within a 12-month period, you'll earn one free.

**Ask if there's a cash discount.**

> Some service providers will offer a discount if you pay in cash (otherwise they're paying credit card fees.) It never hurts to ask!

## Save with DIY Grooming

*Do-it-yourself dog grooming might sound a little intimidating at first but just think about it for a minute. Unlike cutting your spouse's or your children's hair, you'll never have to worry that you've done it just right (unless yours is a show dog). No one will laugh at your dog for an uneven haircut! Also, you can do as much or as little grooming as you like, learning some DIY skills such as dog washing while leaving some tasks you don't want to do, whether hair cutting or nail trimming, to the pros.*

**Try self-serve dog washes.**

For about $15, you can rent a self-service dog wash facility with a special deep sink (many surrounded with special ramps so you're not bending over your dog and breaking your back), shampoos and conditioners, towels, brushes, dog dryers, and more.

Along with saving your back, another big benefit is you won't have all that dog hair going down your drain (no cleanup!)

**Look for DIY dog washes at your car wash.**

A growing number of car wash businesses are offering special stalls especially outfitted for dog bathing, many similar to the DIY self-serve dog washes at grooming salons.

We've seen a variety of prices starting at $5 to $10. Some offer a low-cost package if you bring all your own supplies while offering a costlier package if you use their supplies, ranging from shampoo to towels. Some washes even offer a vacuum service to quickly dry your dog's hair.

**Use your old brushes.**

Yes, you'll find many, many dog brushes of all kinds on the market and they work great. Pin brushes are great for wiry coats, slicker brushes are recommended for heavily shedding dogs. But guess what…your old human brush works wonders, too.

Our dogs love to be brushed with our old hairbrushes (maybe it's the scent). They may not do as good a job as the specialty brushes but, since the dogs enjoy it, we brush them far more often and that's the real key to successful brushing!

**Make your own grooming apron.**

Don't have a waterproof apron for bathing and grooming your dog? Save your old shower curtains, cut holes for your head and arms.

No old shower curtain? Grab a large trash bag, add a neck and two arm holes, and you're ready to go. It might not win any fashion awards but it makes for a quick and easy cleanup!

**Dilute your dog shampoo.**

Dog shampoo is concentrated so you can dilute with much as ¼ water to ¾ shampoo and still have plenty of cleaning power. One way to make your shampoo go further is to "prewash" your dog using a super diluted mixture. We mix just a few drops of dog shampoo in a gallon jug and shake it up. We then pour this mix over our dog (especially our hound-lab mix Irie who has greasy, dense hair). Next, follow with a traditional bath. This prewash breaks up the oil and saturates the hair so you'll get a better, more efficient wash when you shampoo.

**Do your own FURminator treatments.**

Many groomers offer a FURminator® treatment for dogs as a lower-cost option to shampooing and clipping. The FURminator® treatment begins with a low-shed shampoo followed by a FURminator solution to help release the undercoat that needs to come out followed by a rinse and a high-velocity dryer before brushing your dog with a FURminator.

You can save money by giving your dog a very similar treatment at home, paying for your FURminator and solutions in just a few home treatments.

**Invest in nail clippers.**

Unlike some special dog grooming tools that you can substitute with items you already have on hand, it pays to invest in good nail clippers made especially for dogs.

You'll have your choice of types. Guillotine-style clippers look almost like scissors but they feature two rounded sections; you'll place the dog's nail in the center of the rounded out sections and squeeze. Scissor-style clippers with a safety arm are also popular.

The most important consideration is that you're comfortable using the clippers and that they cleanly cut the nail and don't fracture it. Trim just a little, being careful to avoid the live "quick" or vein that flows through the middle of the nail; it can be difficult to see on dark nails. The nail will bleed if this is cut and it's very painful to your dog.

**Walk your dog on sidewalks.**

Walking your dog on sidewalks and asphalt will wear down your dog's nails…you might be able to avoid clipping them!

**Cut your dog's hair.**

Cutting your dog's hair can be fun or frustrating, all depending how you approach the task. We've always cut our dogs' hair ourselves and, while there's never been a risk of winning any prizes for grooming, the haircuts do the job. Sure, they occasionally might be a little crooked, sometimes a little choppy, but we've never heard a word of complaint from any of our dogs!

The key is to start with a good, thorough brushing to detangle, then work on one area at a time. Electric clippers are easy to use and, with variable guards, you can clip hair short or long. Scissor cuts are tougher and you'll want to watch for your dog's ears and tongue at all times as well as his eyes.

special tip

*Go slowly when cutting your dog's hair (you can always go back later and trim more), stay in a good mood, and make sure you have plenty of good treats! You'll find many instructional videos on YouTube to help you successfully trim your dog's hair.*

**Take a dog grooming class.**

If you enjoy dog grooming, consider taking a class at a local community college. Not only can you learn to do a great job grooming your own dog, but it can be a money-making skill for you as well!

**Use an old hairdryer.**

Special dog hair dryers are available but you can use an old hair dryer—just be sure to turn the heat down to low. Don't dry your dog's hair on a high heat or you'll burn his skin!

**Buy some clippers.**

Electric hair clippers are inexpensive enough to pay for themselves in just a few haircuts. They're safe (even with a wiggly dog) and easy to use. Again, check YouTube for how-to videos on using clippers.

The key is to go slowly—both in terms of cutting and in terms of letting your dog become accustomed to the sound. We got our Tiki, who has medium-long hair, accustomed to the clippers by turning it on and giving her treats for several sessions—without ever touching her with the clippers.

**Protect your dog's ears.**

Before you start the bathing process, you'll want to put a cotton ball in your dog's ears. It's important not to get water down in the ear canal because this can cause an ear infection that can require a trip to the vet later on and can be uncomfortable for your dog.

**Deskunk with home ingredients.**

Rather than purchasing a more expensive skunk odor eliminator to use the next time your dog gets a little too close to a skunk, you can purchase these inexpensive ingredients to have on hand. Here's what you'll need: two pints of hydrogen peroxide (3 percent solution), a box of baking soda, dishwashing gloves, and a few spoonfuls of dishwashing soap.

When needed, mix the hydrogen peroxide, baking soda, and about two teaspoons of dishwashing soap with one gallon of water.

Gently sponge this mixture over your dog, carefully avoiding his eyes; after four or five minutes, rinse off the solution.

special tip

*It's very important to keep these ingredients in a box in your pantry but do not mix them until you need them. When you're done, discard any unused solution—never store it or it can explode!*

**Make a dry shampoo.**

> You'll find commercial dry shampoos for bathing your dog during the winter or between shampoos but it's easy and inexpensive to make your own dry shampoo at home.
>
> The basic recipe uses one cup of one of these ingredients: cornstarch, flour, baby powder, or unscented talc. Many recipes also call for adding 1/2 cup of baking soda to deodorize and/or a 1/2 cup of salt to help remove dirt.
>
> Don't use any of these mixtures on dogs with skin irritations or cuts. Mix the ingredients and pour in a clean, dry glass jar with a metal, screw-top lid. Close the lid and shake the ingredients to mix then punch about a half dozen holes in the lid. Sprinkle it on your dog, work it down into his hair, then brush it all out—you're done!

## Saving on Other Dog Services

*With some creative thinking and some help from dog-loving neighbors and friends, you can cut costs on other dog services as well.*

**Form a dog walking coop.**

> If you've been hiring a dog walker in the past, get together with fellow dog lovers in your neighborhood to form a dog walking coop.
>
> By taking turns, you'll have the chance to have free time while your dog is walked, and he'll have the social interaction with other dogs.

**Buy a multi-day doggie day care package.**

Some doggie day cares offer a multi-day package so you can perhaps buy 10 days of doggie day care for the price of eight or nine. You'll use the days as you like.

**Create your own dog park with friends.**

Do you and a couple of neighbors have fenced yards and dogs that enjoy each other's company? Arrange a play date every week for your dogs to enjoy some fun play time—saving you a drive to the dog park.

**Check dog festivals for discount pet photos.**

Check for dog-centric festivals in your area; many feature professional photographers doing mini photo sessions. These low-cost sessions can give you great photos—and often they benefit local shelters and rescues!

**Learn some pet photography skills.**

Is the cost of pet photography out of your budget? With today's digital cameras, you can pick up pet photography skills without spending anything other than time—and that's all time spent with your dog.

Head to the library for some pet photography books for helpful tips on posing, lighting, and capturing your dog's unique personality.

# 5 Dog Expenses to Never Cut

We're all for trimming expenses whenever you can—but there are some dog expenditures you should never cut. These include:

1. **Spay and Neuter.** Think you can save money by not spaying or neutering your dog? Think again. Besides the substantial cost of an unplanned litter, an increased risk of health problems also looms for unaltered pets.

2. **Quality Dog Food.** You can save money on your dog's food by searching for coupons and special offers, not by reducing the quality of his food.

3. **Core Vaccines.** The core vaccines—distemper, adenovirus, parvovirus and rabies—are the necessary vaccines (and, in the case of rabies, mandatory). Make sure your dog is current on these immunizations for his health and safety.

4. **Heartworm Preventative.** Heartworm preventative isn't cheap–but it's cheaper and much safer than treatment for heartworms. Don't stop giving heartworm preventative without talking to your vet first; in some parts of the country, heartworms are a year-around risk.

5. **Annual Wellness Exam.** An annual exam—even if your dog's not due for shots—is important for catching any health problems early, when treatment is most successful and least expensive.

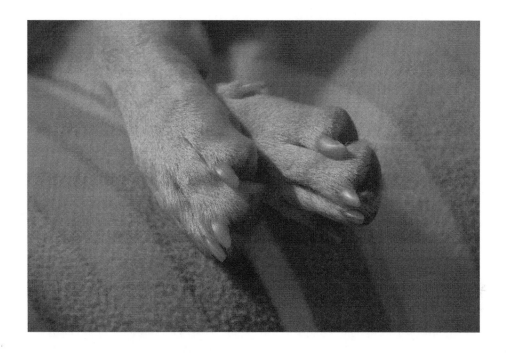

# Veterinary Care

Health doesn't have to equal wealth when it comes to your dog's veterinary care. Much of the savings you can reap can be gained through preventative care, making sure your dog stays healthy by keeping him well-fed and exercised.

When it comes time for routine veterinary care, there are some steps you can take to trim costs but, in general, this is one area where you want to invest; your dog's wellness exam and immunizations will *save* you money in the long run.

However, when faced with the necessity for sudden emergency care, it's not always advisable or even possible to consider costs. When rushing your pet to the emergency veterinary clinic in the middle of the night your main priority, of course, is to secure the quickest and best treatment for them, not saving a few dollars.

Still, there are strategies you can follow to prepare for the possibility of these emergencies in advance and so perhaps to mitigate some of the costs associated with them.

In a nutshell, the best way to avoid these situations is to keep them from arising in the first place. By keeping your dog healthy and in a secure environment, you can decrease the chances of these emergencies happening to your pet.

## Must-Dos that Save You Money

*You know that saying that sometimes you have to spend money to make money? Well, in the case of your dog's health, sometimes you have to spend money to save money down the line. There are some expenses that you want to make sure you* don't *cut in these tough times because these expenditures will save you money later.*

### Schedule an annual exam.

Sadly, some people are trying to trim dog costs by skipping their dog's annual exam. This can result in more veterinary expenditures and it's definitely not the place to trim costs.

Remember, your dog ages faster than you do; that annual exam is similar to you visiting your doctor every seven years. If you skip a few years, you are putting your dog at risk of dangerous—and expensive—health problems. It's less expensive and much better for your dog to visit the vet every year!

**Spay and neuter.**

Spaying or neutering your dog will result, not only in a happier dog that's not trying to get out to breed (running the risk of getting lost, hurt, or in fights) and creating unwanted litters, but in a healthier dog as well.

Spaying a female dog will reduce her risk of breast cancer and completely eliminate her risk of uterine and ovarian cancer. Neutering your male dog has many health benefits for him as well, including preventing testicular cancer and prostate problems. Neutering can also help him avoid hernias and perianal tumors.

**Brush your dog's teeth.**

Good dental care can save you hundreds of dollars in cleaning fees and it helps keep your dog healthier. Try to brush your dog's teeth several times per week using a special toothpaste and toothbrush designed for dogs; the toothpaste has a flavor such as beef or poultry, and it is not a problem if he swallows it.

special tip

*Never use human toothpaste when brushing your dog's teeth! It contains fluoride which is toxic to your dog. If you don't have special dog toothpaste, just use a plain toothbrush (and dip it in chicken broth to make it a little more popular!)*

**Keep your dog's ears clean.**

If you can avoid needing an ear swab on your next vet visit, that's $35 saved…not to mention the cost of medication! Our dog Irie has droopy ears that need frequent cleaning but we also check our dog Tiki's ears to make sure they're clean—and to make certain no tick has found its way into her ear.

To clean your dog's ears, use a very soft cloth or a cotton ball, wet it with an ear-cleaning solution, and gently rub the flaps clean. We check our dogs' ears every week.

However, be careful not to clean too deep inside because the ear is extremely tender and going too far inside can cause pain. And be sure not to use a Q-tip or any sharp cleaning object because you can easily damage your dog's ear canal if poked too hard.

You can make your own ear cleaning solution with two parts white vinegar and one part water (or a one to one mix); don't use it if your dog's ear has any cuts or sores or it will burn.

**Compare spay and neuter costs.**

Spay and neuter costs vary by veterinarian's office and with the size of your dog as well. In general, look for neutering to cost about $150-$170. Spaying runs about $200 for dogs under 40 pounds and about $250 for dogs over 40 pounds.

Your dog will also need to have had a recent physical exam and pre-anesthetic blood testing at most clinics, which runs about $50. (Remember, if you get your dog at a shelter, many will already have been spayed or neutered, a real savings!)

**Assemble a first aid kit for your dog.**

A dog emergency kit is a must for every house. In fact, you should assemble pet first aid kits both for your car and your home. VCA Animal Hospitals' Dr. Donna J. Spector, DVM, DACVIM (you might have seen her on *The Ellen DeGeneres* show!) recommends these items when making a First Aid Kit for dogs and cats:

- **Phone numbers and directions on laminated (waterproof) paper**—for owner's home, veterinary clinic, emergency clinic, and poison control center.

- **Equipment and supplies**—muzzle, restraints, collar/leash, scissors, flea comb, tweezers, pliers/hemostats, magnifying glass, nail clippers, penlight or flashlight, paper towels, towels, tourniquet, cotton swabs, cotton balls, bandage material, bandage tape, eye dropper, oral syringe, thermometer, lubricating jelly, disposable/latex gloves, ice cream sticks or yardstick (which may be used as splints), emergency ice and heat packs, liquid dish soap, and saline solution (for rinsing wounds).

- **Nutritional Support**—rehydrating solution (Pedialyte, etc) and sugar solution (Karo syrup, etc). Keep a collapsible bowl in the first aid kit.

- **Medications**—activated charcoal, alcohol, Betadine/Nolvasan, eye rinse, triple antibiotic ointment, ophthalmic (eye) ointment, hydrogen peroxide, Benadryl (diphenhydramine), cortisone spray/ointment, sterile saline, antidiarrheal liquid or tablets, flea and tick prevention and treatment, styptic powder, and ear cleaning solution. Always include any prescription medications your pet may be taking.

Dr. Spector recommends that you check your kit frequently for expired products and restock as needed. Be sure to pay close attention to the expiration dates on the hydrogen peroxide and antibiotic ointments, and ask your veterinarian for advice on other first aid kit contents specifically for your pet. And don't forget: tuck your new pet first aid kit in a waterproof plastic container for safekeeping!

**Learn first aid so you can treat minor problems and recognize major problems.**

First aid classes for dog lovers are often taught at local community colleges and sometimes dog-related businesses. For about $60-$90, you can take a one-day class that will help you deal with minor problems you can handle at home, recognize which problems you must handle immediately, and stabilize your dog in an emergency situation so you can rush him to the vet.

To find classes in your area, call your local shelter, talk with local dog businesses, and search for "dog first aid classes" and your city's name.

**Continue heartworm prevention.**

Think you can save money by cutting out heartworm prevention? Think again. Treatment of heartworms is far more expensive than monthly preventative (not to mention the danger of heartworms and treatment to your dog). Before you decide that you can skip any months of prevention, talk to your veterinarian. Some areas are at risk for mosquitoes and therefore for heartworms year around. Also, if you'll be traveling with your dog to warmer area during the winter months, you'll need to continue prevention.

**Buy a dog medical guide.**

Just as a pediatric medical guide helps you to know whether that symptom should mean a trip to the emergency room or if it can wait for a doctor's visit the next day, a dog medical guide can help you identify which problems necessitate a trip to the veterinary emergency clinic.

# Working with Your Vet

*Veterinarians know the tough financial times their clients are facing these days so it pays to work with your vet to come up with a way to keep your dog healthy on your budget. Be up front with your vet about your need to shop online for dog medications, if that's the case, and get her opinion and guidance on what's best for your dog.*

**Explain your financial situation to your vet.**

> Your vet doesn't want to hear about your specific bank balance but be honest about budget restrictions. Ask for your vet's ideas in holding down costs. Are some procedures or immunizations optional? Could the procedures be spaced out over a few months? Does your vet offer payment options?

**Ask for a written estimate.**

> When you're faced with costly veterinary costs such as surgery, ask for a written estimate from your vet. This is helpful at an emotional time when you're worried about your dog and might misunderstand the totals. It's also helpful if you need to get a second opinion and an estimate from another vet.

**Ask about 3-year immunization schedules.**

> The American Animal Hospital Association (AAHA), the only organization that accredits animal hospitals throughout the U.S. and Canada, issued guidelines in 2006 that changed the way some dog owners looked at the frequency of immunizations. Formerly vaccinations were automatically given every year.
>
> AAHA recommends giving your dog an initial series of core vaccines while he's a puppy, followed by a booster at one year of age. After that time, the AAHA Canine Vaccine Guidelines

recommend that distemper, adenovirus and parvovirus core vaccines be administered once every three years.

The frequency of the rabies booster will be locally mandated; some places require annual boosters while others require boostering every three years. As for noncore vaccines such as kennel cough, AAHA recommends, "Noncore vaccinations should be administered whenever the risk of the disease is significant enough to override any risk of vaccination."

**Ask about titer tests.**

Titer tests check the antibody levels in your dog's blood so you may be able to extend the time between immunizations even further (although rabies will still need to be given on your locally-mandated schedule). The price on titer tests has gone down but it's not inexpensive; shop around because rates do vary from vet to vet.

**Ask your vet for grooming suggestions.**

On your next annual vet visit, ask your vet if you should be doing anything differently in terms of your dog's grooming. Should you be trimming your dog's nails more often? Trimming his ear hair? Using a different type of shampoo to help his skin? Small changes to your grooming routine can spell big savings by preventing future problems.

**Research using free vet information services.**

*The Merck Veterinary Manual* has been used by vet professionals for half a century and it's available for free use online at *www.merckvetmanual.com*. You can research your dog's illness or condition to be able to ask the best questions on your next visit with your vet.

**Watch and learn from your vet.**

When your vet and vet techs work with your dog, watch and learn the procedures. When your dog gets his ears cleaned, ask them to show you how it's done.

The same holds true if your dog frequently needs his anal glands expressed. OK, it's not pleasant, but this is man's best friend we're talking about here! If it's a persistent problem for your dog, your vet can teach you how to express your dog's anal glands, a simple procedure which involves a gauze pad and a quick squeeze, saving you about $10-$15 (and far more than that should they become impacted.)

**Ask about collecting samples.**

If your dog needs to be tested for roundworm or intestinal problems, ask your vet if you can bring in a fresh fecal sample obtained that same day; use an inverted, clean zippered sandwich bag to catch the stool before it hits the ground, if possible.

Similarly, ask about obtaining a fresh urine sample in a clean jar to save that sample fee.

**Avoid emergency vet visits with preemptive care.**

Does your dog seem sick on Friday afternoon? Don't wait until the vet's office closes for the weekend; run him by for a quick office visit if possible. The price of a routine office visit is far lower than the cost of an emergency vet visit.

If there is a problem, it's better for your dog's health to take care of the problem sooner rather than later; if not, you've put your mind at rest with a less expensive vet visit.

**Plan procedures with the weekend in mind.**

Does your dog need spaying or neutering? Anesthesia for a dental cleaning? Schedule non-emergency care with the idea of the vet's office being closed over the weekend. If you can, schedule the procedure early in the week if someone can be home with your dog upon his return.

Although it's nice to pick up a dog on Friday and be home with him over the weekend, if you have questions about his recovery over the weekend, it can be difficult to reach your vet's office. If problems arise during off hours, emergency vet care is more costly than a quick office visit to your regular vet.

**Keep your dog's vet records.**

Whether your vet's office closes or you move to another city, you'll want your dog's veterinary history. Although in most cases you'll be able to obtain a copy, it helps to keep a copy at home to avoid repeating vaccinations you might have been able to wait another year or two before boostering. Those records are also invaluable if you should need to suddenly evacuate with your pet or take your dog to an emergency vet in the middle of the night.

**Follow up on emergency care at your vet.**

Although a late-night or weekend injury or illness may necessitate a trip to the emergency vet, see if follow-up visits can be made at your regular vet's office for cost savings.

**Ask about vet payment plans.**

If you are hit with unexpected vet bills, it doesn't hurt to ask about payment plans. Many offer affordable plans so you can split the cost of treatment over a period of months.

**Shop around for a vet.**

All vets do not charge the same fees. Especially if you have a new dog and don't yet have a vet or you're moving to a new city, it pays to make a few calls and ask the cost of their basic office visit. Some areas report that veterinary offices outside major metropolitan areas charge lower rates than their big city counterparts.

## Low-Cost Options

*You might have to make a few calls to find low-cost options in your area, but you can find low-cost vaccination clinics, microchipping, and spay/neuter clinics. Some are open to everyone; some clinics are for those who can prove financial need.*

**Look for low-cost vaccination clinics.**

Look for low-cost vaccination clinics in your area—our local grocery store hosts them in the parking lot every month. These are often held on weekends in mobile clinics, at area shelters, and at pet festivals.

Prices are often partially subsidized by governmental agencies or by local kennel clubs and rescue organizations. Prices typically run around $15 for worming treatments, from $6 to $25 for rabies injections, and $15 to $35 for Distemper/Hepatitis/Parvo vaccinations.

Other vaccinations such as for Bordatella and Lyme disease and testing for heartworms are sometimes offered as well. It's probably a good idea to bring along your pet's license, previous vaccination certificate, or other documentation; many clinics require it. Events generally require that your dog be on a leash.

107

**Look for low-cost dog license options.**

As with low-cost vaccination clinics, you'll also find some
opportunities for low-cost dog licenses if required by your city.
Check local pet expos and ask your local animal care department
if there are any opportunities coming up for free or discounted
dog licenses. We recently attended a pet expo in San Antonio and
residents brought in their dogs for free city licenses (and low-cost
immunizations).

Also, many cities offer license discounts for microchipped dogs
(and some cities now use the microchip in lieu of a dog license).
Some cities also charge an intact dog fee, another good reason
(joining both veterinary and behavioral reasons) to have your dog
neutered or spayed!

**Check LuvMyPet.com.**

Since 1976, LuvMyPet has operated low-cost vaccination clinics
on weekends at many locations across the U.S. Along with dog
vaccines, they also offer low-cost microchipping, heartworm and
flea preventative, and cat immunizations.

**Find out if your city has a low-cost clinic.**

Just like low-cost health clinics for humans, many communities
have low-cost animal clinics. Ask your local shelter if your town
has such a clinic where you can obtain discounted spaying and
neutering as well as immunizations (and sometimes the shelter
itself offers a low-cost veterinary clinic, either full- or part-time.)

**Visit a teaching hospital.**

This isn't an option for everyone but, depending on your location,
you may have a veterinary teaching hospital in the region that can

help with major health problems and treatments at a lower cost than through a veterinary clinic.

Check the American Veterinary Medical Association, *www.avma.org*, and *www.VeterinarySchools.com* to see if there are veterinary colleges in your area.

VeterinarySchools.com also offers listings of vet tech programs by state; these schools may be able to help with routine and non-routine care.

**Look for alternatives such as shelter spaying.**

Animal shelters sometimes offer mobile clinics with low-cost spaying and neutering and occasionally, other services such as annual vaccinations. Call your local shelters and ask if they offer some veterinary services.

**Give vaccinations yourself—or not.**

Although the rabies vaccine must always be given by your veterinarian, other immunizations can be purchased online at companies such as Drs. Foster and Smith (*www.drsfostersmith.com*) and Revival (*www.revivalanimal.com*) and shipped directly to you.

However, giving immunizations at home is trickier than it might seem. One problem is that vaccines are now sold in vials, not by individual shots, so unless you have many dogs, the vaccine may go bad before it's used.

Also, you'll need to purchase needles and syringes (which should only be used once), mix the vaccines in many cases, fill the syringes, and give the shot. (Do you know how to give a subcutaneous or an intramuscular injection... and know the difference?)

An easier and more economical solution for most people is to search for low-cost vaccine clinics.

Another good reason to forego the home immunization route: there is a danger of anaphylactic shock with immunizations, a problem that can be addressed instantly if the vaccine is being given at a vet's office but one that could be fatal if you're giving the immunization at home.

## Check into Discounts

*Discount programs can help you save at the veterinarian's office but sometimes you won't know about those discounts unless you ask.*

**Look at veterinary discount programs.**

> Unlike pet insurance, a discount program like PetAssure (*www.petassure.com*) or United Pet Care (*www.unitedpetcare.com*) offers you discounts on veterinary expenditures. These types of programs accept dogs regardless of pre-existing conditions, age, or hereditary disease.
>
> The discount is taken at the veterinarian's office (only veterinarians within the network), and there are no deductibles. Generally all medical procedures are included but items such as flea preventative and lab work done outside the vet's office may or may not be covered.
>
> The savings can be well worth the cost. For example, United Pet Care is presently priced at $12.99 per month; your discount is 50

percent or more on all office visits and medications dispensed by
your vet are discounted 20-25 percent.

**Ask about special discounts.**

Ask your vet if she offers any special discounts (it never hurts to
ask!) Veterinarians offer a variety of discounts: senior citizen,
firefighters, military, full-time student, etc. (Also, some
communities offer senior discounts on dog licenses.)

**Ask about multiple pet discounts.**

Some veterinary offices offer a multiple pet discount if you have
more than one dog or cat. (And, if you're shopping around for a
new vet, this is another question to ask if yours is a multi-pet
household!)

**Keep an eye out for discounts related to certain months such as pet
dental health month.**

Just like human health care, certain months are promotional times
for certain types of canine health issues: dental health, obesity,
and more. February is Pet Dental Month and many clinics run
related specials during this month while Pet Wellness Month in
October can bring wellness visit promotions, discounted
immunizations, etc.

## Asking for Help

*When faced with a major veterinary bill, many dog lovers have to ask for
help during these tough times. Your veterinarian is your first resource;
she'll know of programs her clients have used. You'll need patience and
persistence to find money in this economy; many programs are short on*

*donations and they've have had to limit their assistance programs. Keep*
*trying!*

**Establish a relationship with your vet.**

If your dog undergoes an emergency or serious illness, you may
need to set up a payment plan with your vet for expensive
treatment. This is only a potential option if you're a customer
who has been shown to do business with the veterinarian's office.
It pays to establish a relationship with one vet rather than
popping into a different office each visit.

**Look into CareCredit.**

CareCredit (*www.carecredit.com*) is a credit card specifically for
health care costs including veterinary care. This card has a low
monthly payment option. It offers a no interest payment plan if
you pay in full within 6, 12, 18 or 24 months on purchases with
your CareCredit card.

There are no up-front charges to pay your vet before treatment
can commence; the treatments are charged to your credit card.
The length of time you have to pay off your balance depends on
which promotional payment plan you choose when you use the
card.

**Look into ChaseHealth Advance veterinary loans.**

Chase Health (*www.chasehealthadvance.com*) provides no-
interest payment plans for 3, 6, 12, 18 and 24 months with no
down payment and no application fee. Lines of credit start at
$5,000 and can be used to cover major and minor surgery,
emergency care, dental care, arthritis treatments, ear surgery, and
more.

**Look into regional assistance programs.**

The Humane Society of the United States has an extensive list of assistance programs in the US and Canada available to residents of the area. Check *www.humanesociety.org* (search for "trouble affording pet") for a list of programs that offer a variety of services including pet food, spaying and neutering services, vaccination assistance, veterinary care, temporary foster care, and more for dog lovers in financial stress.

**Look into breed-specific veterinary care assistance programs.**

Some breed-specific programs can help provide assistance with the cost of veterinary care. Each group has specific rules so check your group's website for details.

If you don't see an assistance program for your dog's breed, check the American Kennel Club website, *www.akc.org*, for contacts for breed groups that can steer you toward appropriate assistance groups. Breed assistance groups include:

- Boston terrier: *www.bostonrescue.net*
- Corgi: *www.corgiaid.org*
- Doberman: *www.doberman911.org*
- Golden retriever: *www.grca-nrc.org*
- Labrador retriever: *www.labmed.org* and *www.labradorlifeline.org*
- Pit Bull (serving American Pit Bull Terriers, American Staffordshire Terriers, Staffordshire Bull Terriers, and pit bull mixes): *www.pbrc.net/fund/financial.html*
- Small Terriers (Scotties, Westies, Cairn, Norwich, Norfolk, etc): *www.welcome.to/dougalsfund*
- Tibetan Spaniel: *www.tstrust.org*
- West Highland White Terrier: *www.westiemed.org*

**Apply for financial assistance from pet-related nonprofits.**

Several nonprofit organizations specialize in offering financial assistance to pet owners. Check with:

- **AAHA Helping Pets Fund** *www.aahahelpingpets.org* This arm of the American Animal Hospital Association provides assistance for emergency and non-elective treatment of abandoned pets and pets whose owners are facing financial hardship.

- **Angels4Animals** *www.angels4animals.org* This nonprofit's program Guardian Angel works directly with veterinary clinics to help provide assistance to pet lovers who are facing euthanization or surrendering of a pet because of financial limitations.

- **Brown Dog Foundation** *www.browndogfoundation.org* This nonprofit works with pet owners in temporary financial strain who are seeking veterinary help for their pets for a treatable but life-threatening illness.

- **Canine Cancer Awareness** *caninecancerawareness.org* This nonprofit helps pet owners who cannot pay for canine cancer treatment; payments go directly to vets.

- **Cody's Club** *codysclub.bravehost.com* This fund assists pet lovers in paying for canine radiation treatments; payments are made directly to vets for radiation.

- **Help-A-Pet** *www.help-a-pet.org* Help-A-Pet specializes in providing financial assistance to help the pets of senior citizens, physically and mentally challenged individuals, and children of the working poor.

- **IMOM.org** *www.imom.org* IMOM provides funding for non-routine veterinary care for companion animals.

- **Jake Brady Memorial Fund** *www.myjakebrady.com* This fund works to help seniors, physically and mentally challenged adults, low-income families, and unemployed individuals who are having difficulties paying for non-routine veterinary help.

- **The Mosby Foundation** *www.themosbyfoundation.org* Financial assistance for life-saving emergency veterinary care is the focus of this foundation.

- **The Pet Fund** *www.thepetfund.com* The Pet Fund is not for emergency care but is aimed at providing assistance for costs beyond the normal expenses of vaccination, spay and neuter surgeries, food and routine veterinary care.

- **United Animal Nations LifeLine Grants** *www.uan.org* The LifeLine Individual Grant is designed to help pets with a responsible owner who cannot afford the cost of urgent and lifesaving care. This organization also offers the LifeLine Rescue Grant to help a rescued animal that has been taken from a life-threatening situation within the past month. For people who have been struck by personal disaster, ranging from domestic violence to house fires to natural disasters, they offer LifeLine Crisis Relief for individuals to help with the cost of pet care.

## Pet Insurance

Like human health insurance, pet insurance helps you pay for treatment in case of accidents or illness. Modern veterinary care has progressed to offer treatments—sometimes expensive ones—for diseases and conditions that previously might have been untreatable. A growing number of companies offer pet insurance as an optional employee benefit to their workers and an increasing number of pet lovers (although still a minority) are opting to cover their dogs with pet insurance.

Just as when shopping for your own insurance, you'll find many options when looking for pet insurance—from accident-only coverage all the way to comprehensive coverage that pays for annual visits and vaccines. In between, rates and the amount of coverage varies with sliding scales of deductibles and factors that range from where you live to the age and breed of your dog.

Whether or not to cover your dog through pet insurance is a decision only you can make. Some choose to "self-insure," putting aside money monthly in a savings account to cover future veterinary bills. Others opt to take out a policy with a high deductible, one that would assist only in a costly illness or accident.

**Compare pet insurance plans.**

> Like any other insurance policy, pet insurance plans vary widely in everything from exclusions to deductibles. In selecting a pet insurance plan, though, take the time to read the fine print. You'll want to ask:
>
> - What is the deductible? (Some plans will offer different deductible levels; the higher your deductible, the lower your monthly premium.)
>
> - What percentage of my claim will be reimbursed? Eighty to ninety percent is typical on many policies.
>
> - What is covered? Find out just what the policy covers— *before* you need coverage for it.

- What's excluded? Pre-existing conditions are generally excluded from coverage—so don't wait until you need insurance to try to obtain it. However, some companies also exclude for "hereditary and congenital conditions" so find out exactly what their definition of this is.

  For example, some policies exclude hip dysplasia. Others offer additional riders for hip dysplasia while some policies cover it unless it was a pre-existing condition.

- Are there breed-specific exclusions that might include my dog? For example, we've seen policies that exclude glaucoma in Beagles, Siberian huskies and Welsh Springer spaniels and epilepsy in Beagles, Belgian Tervurens, dachshunds, German shepherds, golden retrievers, keeshonds and Labrador retrievers.

- Does this plan include ongoing conditions such as epilepsy or diabetes? Some insurance plans have separate riders for ongoing conditions.

- Does this plan cover specialist care such as opthalmologists or dermatologists?

- Will my premiums rise with my dog's age?

- What's the discount for multiple pets?

- Does this policy include prescription medications? What about prescription diets?

- What's the limitation *per incident*?

- Is there an *annual* cap on benefits?

- What's the *lifetime* limit on benefits?

- Can I use my own veterinarian or do I need to visit a network vet?

- Does this policy cover my dog while he's traveling with me?

- Does this plan cover a visit to an emergency veterinary clinic?

- Does this plan cover any holistic care? Acupuncture?

**Make the decision to insure (or not) early.**

If you do decide to insure your dog, shop around first but be sure to insure your pet as soon as possible. Most companies won't insure a pet with a pre-existing condition.

Also, premiums are lower the younger your dog is—and, at some companies, your premiums will lock in at that lower rate. Dogs insured younger than one year of age are also eligible for coverage for some conditions such as hip dysplasia that might otherwise be excluded.

**Check out accident-only policies.**

Accident-only policies are another option for pet insurance. These are lower priced than traditional insurance policies and only cover costly accident care.

**Learn about pet insurance discounts.**

Does your pet insurance company offer a discount for prepaying for an entire year? Some do and the savings can be as much as 25 percent.

**Ask about employee discounts.**

Learn if you're entitled to any special pet insurance discounts through your employer or union. For example, members of the American Federation of State, County and Municipal Employees offers Union Plus Pet Health Insurance to its members as well as Union Plus Pet Savings program, a pet health care savings program.

**Look for discounts on pet insurance.**

Even if you don't have a discount through your employer, you may have other memberships that qualify you for a discount. For example, Sam's Club presently offers its members a 5 percent discount on the annual premium for Veterinary Pet Insurance (VPI) . Kroger grocery stores offer customers pet insurance through PetFirst Healthcare®.

**Ask about pet wellness plans.**

Ask your vet clinic if it offers a pet wellness plan. Many corporate veterinary offices (such as Banfield) offer these plans and a growing number of private veterinary practices—and holistic vets—offer similar wellness plans.

Unlike insurance, these plans are focused on preventative care, offering it at a discount; some, such as Banfield's "Optimum Wellness Plan," then offer a free finance option in the event of costly veterinary expenditures beyond routine care.

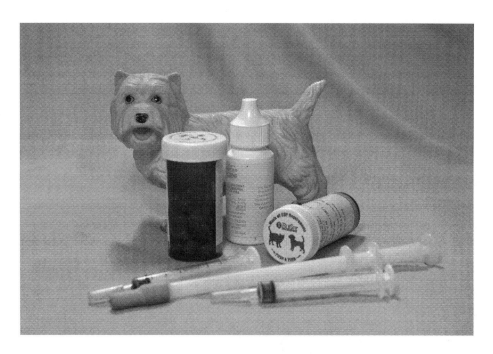

# Prescriptions & Medications

Pet prescriptions and over the counter medications account for a big portion of many dog budgets. From heartworm and flea preventatives all the way to prescriptions for short-term illnesses and chronic conditions, pet medications are a necessity.

Just as with buying good quality dog food, you want to be sure that you're buying good quality pet medications—otherwise you are wasting your money and endangering your dog's health.

In this chapter, we point out ways to save at your veterinarian's office, at your local drugstore, and at reputable online pharmacies.

# Buying from Your Vet

*Buying pet prescriptions from your vet is convenient; your vet writes a prescription and, as you check out, your prescription is filled. However, with some pre-trip preparation, you can save money. Also, be upfront with your vet: explain that you're trying to save money and ask if she has suggestions for saving on this prescription?*

**Ask about matching drug prices.**

> Before you head to the vet's office, do some online research (at reputable online veterinary supply companies, *not* on Craigslist or eBay), as to the price of heartworm preventative and other medication you know you'll need. Be sure to take into account shipping you'd pay, too. Print out the product page and take it to your vet's office and ask if they can match (or come close to) the online price.

**Buy preventatives in bulk.**

> Often it's less expensive to buy a full year's worth of flea or heartworm preventative rather than purchasing just a six-month supply. If your dog is no longer a puppy and not growing, it can pay to invest in a year's supply.

**Look for coupons.**

> Think coupons aren't for pet medications? Think again. We've found $5 rebates on heartworm preventative online; we just printed it out and took it to our vet's office for their signature when we bought the medication. If you know you'll be buying heartworm preventative from your vet, check out the preventative's website *before* your scheduled vet visit to look for coupons and rebate forms.

# Buying at the Drugstore

*Hundreds of pet prescriptions can be purchased at your local drugstore with your veterinarian's prescription. You'll be able to take advantage of the savings offered at large drug stores including their discount programs.*

**Fill your dog's prescription at your drugstore.**

> Can your dog's prescription be filled at your drugstore? Many can and often at a great savings (and you'll have the option of generic, low-cost equivalents for some drugs.) Find out!

**Learn if your county belongs to NACo.**

> The National Association of Counties (NACo), *www.naco.org*, offers a prescription drug discount card for residents without prescription drug coverage or if your prescription isn't covered by insurance—and that includes your pet's prescriptions, too. There's no fee but your county must belong to the association; about half the counties in the US belong to the association and almost 60,000 pharmacies accept the card.

**Check drugstore prescription clubs.**

> Some drugstores offer prescription clubs for lower costs. For example, the Walgreens Prescription Savings Club includes discounted pricing on many common pet prescriptions such as Amoxicillin (antibiotic), Humulin® (insulin), Hydrocortisone (skin conditions), Omeprazole (digestive), and more.
>
> To qualify for the discount, you'll need a valid prescription for your pet from your vet and the medication must be one that has a human equivalent.

**Check printable prescription cards.**

Look online for several printable prescription cards acceptable at many traditional pharmacies.

For example, the free Community Discount Drug Card, communitydiscountdrugcard.com, is accepted at over 50,000 drugstores and includes coverage for your pets. Similarly the RXFreeCard (*www.rxfreecard.com)* and PrescriptionDrugs.com (*www.prescriptiondrugs.com*) offer printable prescription cards to cover your pet's medications that can be filled in a traditional pharmacy.

**Don't administer your human medications to your dog.**

Although they may be safe for you, that doesn't mean that your medications—whether prescription or over-the-counter—are safe for your dog. In fact, many can be deadly.

special tip

*To avoid potentially expensive veterinary treatment (or worse), always give your vet a call before giving your dog any human medication.*

**Use your AAA card to help save money on dog prescriptions.**

A benefit to being an American Automobile Association member is the free AAA Prescription Saving Card which can be used any time you fill a prescription that's not covered by insurance— including pet prescriptions filled at drugstores! The average savings is 20 percent with a greater saving on those prescriptions filled by mail.

# Buying Prescriptions and Medications Online

*The convenience of online ordering combined with the ease of comparison shopping makes online pharmacies popular for pet medications. You'll want to make sure that you're buying from a* reputable *pet pharmacy.*

**Know how to identify a reputable online pet pharmacy.**

> Like just about everything else, plenty of pet medicines can be purchased online—but buyer beware. Online, buy *only* from reputable sources (skip those bargain prices you might find through individuals selling through eBay or Craigslist). Reputable pet medicine companies will require veterinary prescriptions for many medications such as heartworm preventative.
>
> How do you know if a company's reputable? The US Food and Drug Administration (FDA) recommends that you look for the Veterinary-Verified Internet Pharmacy Practice (Vet-VIPPS) Sites; these are sites accredited by the National Association of Boards of Pharmacy.
>
> The FDA also recommends that you order only from US-based pharmacies; they have found foreign companies selling unapproved drugs, counterfeit pet drugs and drugs beyond their expiration date.
>
> While pet owners who buy pet meds from these unapproved sites may think they're saving money, the FDA notes, "in reality, they may be short-changing their pet's health and putting its life at risk."

**Order from an outsourced prescription management service that your veterinarian uses.**

The FDA has a money-saving tip for ordering your pet medications online: ask your vet if they order from a prescription management service you could use.

According to the FDA, "These state-licensed Internet pharmacy services work directly with the veterinarian, require that a prescription be written by the veterinarian, and support the veterinarian-client-patient relationship. Ask your veterinary hospital if it uses an Internet pharmacy service."

**Ask your vet about online pharmacies.**

Remember, you're trusting your pet's health to your veterinarian so you want to work *with* your vet to obtain medications, not behind his or her back. Explain that you're watching your money and looking at an online pharmacy as a way to save.

When you ask your vet to write a prescription for your pet's medication, ask for his opinion of the online pharmacy you're considering. Has your vet had a good experience with the site? You'll want your dog's veterinary records to reflect that you're giving medication you've purchased elsewhere (you don't want to run the risk of drug interaction if your vet doesn't realize you are giving another medication at home.)

**Sign up for online newsletters.**

Many online pet pharmacies offer free e-newsletters; look for exclusive offers, online coupons and news of upcoming specials in these newsletters.

# Around the House

In addition to saving on direct costs, you can also save money on some of the tangential expenses of dog ownership. Dogs necessitate some additional housekeeping and cleaning duties, tasks that you can achieve using some common, low-cost items you probably already have around the house.

## Get Proactive

*Accidents that result in expensive trips to the emergency vet for everything from broken bones to removal of swallowed objects can take a real bite out of the budget. The best defense in this case is a good offense—stop those accidents before they happen!*

**Prevent accidents.**

One way to save big bucks on your veterinary bills is to avoid costly accidents, everything from your dog being struck by a car to ingested objects that have to be surgically removed. Preventative care includes training, dog-proofing your home (and that means everything from safeguarding electrical wires to picking up coins off the floor), fencing your yard, and more.

**Prevent poisonings.**

Accidental poisonings are one of the most common reasons for a costly emergency visit to the vet. According to VPI Pet Insurance, the average cost of a claim made for pet poisoning is almost $800.

And the substances behind those accidents? Many are not the poisons you might think. Dogs have eaten everything from human medications to household plants, alcohol to heavy metals (coins, bolts, you name it).

Here's a look at the top items that resulted in poison claims:

- Accidental Ingestion of Medications (pet or human drugs)
- Rodenticide (mouse & rat poison)
- Methylxanthine Toxicity (chocolate, caffeine)
- Plant Poisoning
- Household Chemicals
- Metaldehyde (snail, slug poison)
- Insecticide
- Heavy Metal Toxicity (lead, zinc)
- Toad Poisoning

- Antifreeze Poisoning
- Walnut Poisoning
- Alcohol Toxicity
- Strychnine

**Puppy-proof your home.**

When you introduce a new dog to your house, you'll need to go over it just like you would if you were bringing a baby into your home. Unlike the new baby, though, this puppy is ready to go exploring from day one! Before the new puppy arrives, spend a little time puppy-proofing your home. Here are some common household items that are poisonous to dogs:

- **Medications:** Acetaminophen, Ibuprofen, aspirin, cough and cold syrups, and prescription drugs should all be kept out of the reach of dogs.

- **Indoor Plants:** Some of these can be very dangerous for dogs and should only be kept on a counter high enough so a dog cannot reach it. If you have a large dog, you may want to get rid of these plants altogether. They include: Tulip bulbs, sago palms, poinsettias, philodendrons, daffodils, lily of the valley, and azaleas.

- **Foods:** These foods are dangerous for dogs: chocolate, yeast, grapes, onions, raisins, Macadamia nuts, alcohol, and Xylitol (found most often in sugar-free chewing gum).

- **Insecticides and Poisons:** These should not be kept in the home, but in a locked cabinet or on a high shelf in the garage. This includes rat poison, flea and tick products, and other insecticides.

- **Cleaners:** These are items frequently kept under the kitchen sink. Dog-proof the cabinet so that these items cannot be taken out by your puppy: bleach, detergent, furniture polish, soap, and disinfectants.

- **Chemicals:** Lighter fluid, turpentine, antifreeze, gasoline, glue, paint, solvents, and any type of acids are all no-nos around your puppy.

- **Tobacco:** If you smoke or have a smoking guest, avoid leaving out a pack of cigarettes (or cigarette butts) that can easily be eaten by a dog.

- **Household hazards:** Make sure all the electrical outlets in your home are covered and that there are no extension cords within sight or available for a dog to chew on. All electrical appliances should be turned off or unplugged, and small collectible items you have showcased in your home should be transferred to the top of an open bookshelf or in an enclosed glass closet.

- **Bathroom hazards:** Make sure no bathroom items are left out on the sink or counter. If you have a cabinet under the bathroom sink, ensure it has a safety lock as well.

Once you've puppy-proofed your home, have a look at it from the puppy's viewpoint: down on the floor. Get down on your hands and knees and go through your entire home. You'd be surprised how different the view looks from down there!

**Know if your homeowner's insurance covers dog bites.**

Here's a worry many people don't have…until it's too late: do you know if your homeowner's insurance covers you in case your dog bites someone? This can be an expensive lesson.

According to Frank N. Darras, an insurance lawyer, "Asking if your dog is covered under your homeowners insurance policy may be a strange question to ask, but according to the Journal of American Medical Association, the number of dog bites in America now tops 4.5 million per year. An overwhelming one-third of all homeowner's liability claims are now related to dog bites, equaling about $1 billion in damages, according to the Insurance Information Institute."

Darras says that one type of policy that has become popular is umbrella insurance, designed to give you added liability protection above and beyond the limits of your homeowners plan.

With an umbrella policy, depending on the insurance company, you can add an additional $1 to $5 million in liability protection designed to "kick-in" when the liability on your other current policies has been exhausted.

Decide what your needs are and, if you have pets, Darras says, "it would be a good idea to consider getting an umbrella policy, especially if you have guests over and your dog tends to snap at people. If you don't regularly have people over and your pooch couldn't hurt a fly, it may not be that important."

In short, ask your insurance company–don't wait to have a problem!

**Learn about insurance riders.**

Depending on where you live, you may be required to carry additional insurance based on the breed of your dog. For example, in Ohio, households with pit bull type dogs (and it's up to the officer to determine if the dog is a "pit bull") are required to maintain a minimum of $100,000 in liability insurance.

While homeowner's insurance typically has that coverage, some insurance companies specifically have exclusions so specific dog breeds are not covered.

You'll need to check with your insurance company for the specifics and, if not covered, find a pit bull-friendly insurance company for coverage. (Some good resources are *SaveaBull.com*, *www.take2rescue.com*, and *www.dogbitelaw.com*.)

Ask your insurance company about ways to trim these costs. Some companies recommend getting your dog Canine Good Citizen certification from the American Kennel Club as evidence that your dog is well trained.

The AKC also recommends contacting breed associations for their members' experiences on finding homeowner's or renter's insurance with your dog's breed in mind.

**Save your upholstery.**

Sure, you can buy slipcovers made for your couch or have them custom made but a far (far, far) cheaper solution is to cover your couch with a blanket if you let your dogs up on the couch. We allow our dogs (and cats) on the couch and our solution is to purchase (at the thrift store, natch) blankets in the same color as our dark green couch.

Yes, it takes some looking because you won't find them just any day but, by keeping a constant eye out, we've been able to buy two blankets and one duvet cover in the same shade. We rotate them so one's always on the couch, one's in the laundry, and one's ready to go.

# In the Yard

*A fenced yard is a great way to give your dog some freedom outdoors while keeping him confined to a safe area. While in that yard (or out on your walk), you'll want to take additional precautions with lawn treatments.*

**Choose your fence wisely.**

> Fenced yards and dogs are a natural combination but, if your yard isn't already fenced, it's a big investment. If you'll be putting in a fence for your dog, choose the type wisely. We have a four-foot-high ranch fence (with about 3x5 inch square mesh) which works for our large dogs but would be too porous for small dogs and puppies.

> The most popular (and best-priced) option is chain link fencing; wooden fences are another option and prevent your dog from seeing out in the neighborhood—whether that's a plus or minus depends on your dog. Each of these traditional fences are costlier than an electronic fence but remember that the electronic fence offers no protection in keeping others—whether neighborhood dogs or children—away from your dog. We have coyotes in our area so an electronic fence is definitely out since coyotes could come and go at will.

**Get several fence estimates.**

> As with any other major investment, it pays to shop around before committing to a fencing contractor.

**Opt for a DIY fence.**

> By purchasing materials and installing a dog fence yourself, you can save about 50 percent on the job. It's not an easy job,

however, and can be more difficult if your yard is sloped, requires the moving of hedges or other greenery, or is especially rocky, making it tough to dig fence posts. (We say this from experience, living in a rocky, sloped area.)

**Check on pre-made dog runs.**

Chain link dog runs in a variety of sizes and heights are a less expensive option than having a fence constructed. Although they are not as roomy as a fenced yard, a run is an option if your dog needs it only a few hours a day.

Look on *www.Craigslist.org, www.recycler.com, www.ebayclassifieds.com*, and similar sites for used runs.

special tip

*If you have a small dog or puppy, make sure the gates are square cornered, not round cornered, or your small dog can escape.*

**Save utility bills with a dog door.**

An efficient dog door can save on your air-conditioning and heating bills, reducing the amount of air that escapes each time your dog goes in or out. (Not to mention the wear and tear on you it saves!)

**Avoid pesticides, fertilizers, and insecticides.**

Poisonous pesticides and insecticides can spell real trouble for pets as can many fertilizers. Dogs love to eat grass, even if that grass is sprayed with weed killer, so be wary when you're walking your dog and keep an eye out for flags that indicate a property has recently received a pesticide or fertilizer treatment.

Along with ingesting the poison, there's also the danger of absorbing the poisons through their paw pads.

*If you've been walking where yards may have been chemically treated, be sure to clean your dog's paws when you return home!*

special tip

**Avoid cocoa mulch.**

Another common yard danger is cocoa mulch, made from cocoa bean shells. The mulch is attractive to dogs because it tastes like chocolate but, like chocolate, it's toxic to dogs.

**Use vinegar to kill weeds.**

The greenest options for your yard and garden are kind not just to the environment but to your pocketbook. Rather than an expensive and toxic chemical weed killer, spray unwanted weeds with white vinegar.

# Cleaning Up

*You'll find many cleaning products in the store that are green and some that are specially marketed to pet owners. However, some of the greenest—and cheapest—household cleaners are common items that will only cost you cents per use.*

**Clean with vinegar.**

Both to reduce your impact on the environment—and on your pocketbook, vinegar makes a great all-purpose cleanser in your home. White distilled vinegar is very inexpensive and disinfects as it cleans.

We keep a spray bottle filled with a mix of about 1/3 vinegar and 2/3 water to clean kitchen counters and other surfaces. We mop with vinegar as well, adding about a cup of vinegar to a gallon of warm water (some people also add a couple of drops of dishwashing liquid). Not only does it clean without chemical fumes but you don't need to worry about your pets getting it on their feet.

special tip

*Apple cider vinegar helps deter fleas so we mop the area where the dogs like to sleep with a mixture of apple cider vinegar and water (it also smells better than white vinegar, we think) and add apple cider vinegar to the rinse cycle when we wash their bedding.*

**Use rubber gloves instead of lint rollers.**

We use old dishwashing gloves to wipe down our furniture. (Wonder what to do when you tear a hole in a glove? Here's the answer!)

Put on the glove, wet it and shake it a little, and you're ready to go. Brush off the furniture with your gloved hand and watch the hair roll up. The gloves can be used over and over again.

The process just takes minutes and the hair is ready to pick up and throw away. (We like to toss the hair outside; the birds and squirrels like to use it when they build their nests!)

**Reuse your old towels.**

Old towels are perfect for cleaning paws after a muddy walk. We keep a basket of rolled old towels on the front porch; when we come in from a walk, we tell the dogs it's time to "do paws" and we clean their feet before we head inside. We use a laundry marker to identify the towels so they don't wind up back with the good towels after a trip through the washing machine.

**Remove urine stains inexpensively.**

Baking soda will absorb fresh urine and remove some of the scent. The sooner you can get it on the stain, the better; to use, absorb as much liquid as you can first with paper towels or rags then apply baking soda to the urine stain. Rubbing the area with a dryer sheet can also remove some of the odor.

**Use cornstarch as carpet cleaner.**

To save money when cleaning your carpet, don't buy expensive commercial formulas. Ordinary kitchen cornstarch makes a safe, effective substitute. Just sprinkle dry cornstarch powder on your carpet, leave it for an hour, then vacuum it up, just as you would the commercial product.

Baking soda can also be used in a similar manner to clean your carpets and remove odors.

**Use shaving cream to remove stains.**

Instead of purchasing separate products to clean around the house, it pays to substitute use things you already have on hand. Shaving cream makes an effective cleaner on mirrors, faucets, jewelry, and also works to remove stains from carpets.

# Preventing Pests

*Oh, those pesky pests! Living in a warm weather area, we keep an eye out for ants and fleas year around. With just some simple household products, you can battle these pests safely and cheaply. These solutions are green not only for the environment but for your pocketbook!*

**Prevent ants with vinegar.**

> Vinegar discourages ants so it's a great product to spray around your pet food bowls during the summer months when ants might invade.

**Prevent fleas naturally—and cheaply.**

> Living in the country, we know fleas…but we never buy special flea shampoo for the dogs since regular dog shampoo and water kill fleas. When you soap up your dog, leave the shampoo on a minute or two extra if possible to help kill the fleas on his coat. Also, it helps if you can have your dog sit in the tub of water; many fleas congregate around his tail area and, by sitting in the tub, he'll drown them!

**Attract and kill fleas naturally with a lamp and pan of water.**

> This method won't work if you have young children in the house or pets that roam every room at night. If you don't have small children and you can close off a room from pets at night, try this method for attracting and killing fleas.

> Take a small table lamp and put in on the floor. Beside the lamp, place a shallow pan filled partially with water and a few drops of dishwashing liquid.

At night, turn on the lamp and shut the door. The heat from the lamp will attract the fleas, they'll fall into the slightly soapy water, and drown. (You don't want to use this if the device might have access by small kids or pets because of the danger of the light getting knocked into the water pan.)

**Kill fleas with banana peels.**

Yes, this one sounds a little wacky but banana peels tossed on the floor will kill fleas (we understand it's the potassium in the bananas that does the trick). You might have to tuck the peels away if your dog tries to eat them or place them in rooms your dog doesn't have access to at the time.

This is a cheap, natural way to kill fleas (and think of the fun you'll have making banana pudding and bread!) Once the peels turn black, toss them out and start all over!

**Prevent fleas with rosemary.**

To use rosemary as a flea preventative, begin by making a rosemary mixture. Add one teaspoon of chopped rosemary to near-boiling water to make a tea. Let the mixture simmer then remove from heat to cool. Set it aside for a few hours until it's room temperature.

Next, wash your dog with his normal shampoo. After shampooing, change the water, making it deep enough so his entire body will be immersed. Now, add the rosemary tea (now cool) to the dog's tub and play with your dog in the water for 15 minutes, if possible. When done, take your dog out of the tub and wash your dog again with a gentle shampoo then put him back into the rosemary water for a final rinse. When done, he'll have a flea preventative that smells so nice!

**Wash your dog's bedding.**

One very low cost way to control fleas in your home is to wash your dog's bedding every week (or even more frequently during peak flea periods). Adding apple cider vinegar to the rinse is an inexpensive way to discourage new fleas. Is your dog's bed on a rug that can be laundered? Toss that in the laundry, too! Hang it all out to dry and you won't have the cost of the dryer and your dog bedding will come out smelling fresh as can be.

**Use only flea products for dogs on dogs.**

DON'T try to save money by buying one flea preventative for your dogs and sharing it with your cats; this mistake can be fatal. You must buy a flea preventative for dogs to use on dogs; cats must have a preventative made only for cats!

**Vacuum frequently.**

Fleas are a seasonal problem for all dog owners but, depending on where you live, that season can be a very long one. (Here in Texas, they're just about a year-round problem.) There are many treatments available to keep your dog flea-free but one of the best –and cheapest—ways to keep fleas out of your house and off of your dog is with frequent home vacuuming. Frequent vacuuming will extract the fleas from your carpet as well as any flea eggs that are present.

Be sure to change your vacuum bags more frequently than usual or, even better, use a bagless vacuum you empty (in the outdoor trash) after each use. And think what a clean home you'll have!

# On the Road

Whether or not your dog accompanies you when your travel, there are going to be certain expenses associated with travel. However, with a bit of planning, you can minimize some of these costs without sacrificing your dog's comfort and well-being.

## Boarding Costs

*Boarding your dog during your vacation is a daily expense that you'll need to calculate in your trip budget. You can find some discounts in boarding as well as alternative to boarding such as pet sitting.*

**Form a dog sitting coop.**

Before your next trip out of town, save money on kennel costs or pet sitting fees by forming your own dog sitter coop. You and fellow dog lovers can trade off dog sitting, feeding, providing medication, and giving companionship to dogs whose owners are on the road.

special tip

*What, your friends don't have dogs? Consider trading out babysitting time—or housecleaning, lawn mowing, or house painting—in exchange for dog sitting.*

**Find a family member to pet sit.**

It's not always possible but, if you're lucky, you'll have a family member who will offer to pet sit for you, saving you the cost of a pet sitter or boarding and saving your dog the stress of kennel boarding or having a stranger as a pet sitter.

**Look at pet sitting exchanges.**

No relatives or close friends in the area to call on for pet sitting? Then join together with other pet lovers through sites such as PetWatch Club (*www.petwatchclub.com*), PetSwap USA (*www.petswapusa.com*), and Swap A Dog (*www.swapadog.com*). These organizations bring together pet lovers who are looking for sitters so you can trade out pet sitting duties.

Search for "pet sitter exchange" and "pet sitting exchange" to find other groups and groups specific to your area.

**Watch for hidden fees.**

Some boarding kennels charge a fee for each time they give your dog medication; others do not. Some charge extra to feed your dog a special diet that you've brought yourself; others do not. (It's always easiest on your dog for him to maintain the same diet he usually has at home.)

**Ask about multi-dog discounts.**

Some boarding kennels offer a discount if two dogs from your household share a boarding kennel. Not only can this be comforting to your dogs but it can save you 25 percent or more on your boarding costs. You'll also find kennels that offer multi-dog discounts without the dogs sharing a kennel.

**Avoid holiday boarding if possible.**

Although it's not possible if the purpose of your trip is a holiday reunion or a family gathering, if you're planning a vacation try to avoid holidays.

Boarding costs can be higher, some kennels require a minimum stay—and your own travel expenses will be more costly, too! (Prices at most destinations go down right after the holidays as everyone returns to work and usually stay down until travelers start thinking about Valentine's Day.)

**Ask about partner offers.**

Many larger companies have partnered with other pet care providers to offer their members discounted services. For example, Fetch! Pet Care customers receive a 5 percent discount on VPI Pet Insurance, and AAA members receive a 10 percent discount on Fetch! Pet Care boarding and day care services.

## Traveling with Your Dog

*Taking your dog on vacation comes down to your dog's personality (some dogs would prefer to stay at home while others love to travel) and your trip plans (whether your dog would be able to accompany you on most activities or would need to be kenneled). If you travel with your dog, plan to do plenty of research before your vacation to book hotels that accept pets (and accept dogs of your dog's size and breed) and save money at the same time.*

**Watch for nonrefundable hotel fees.**

Although they say they're "pet friendly," many hotels charge a "non-refundable pet deposit"—in other words, a fee. When comparing hotel costs, be sure to find out if "deposits" are refundable or not.

**Clarify per night or per stay fees.**

Hotels that charge pet fees may charge per night or per stay. If you'll be staying for multiple days, this fee structure will make a real difference in the cost of your trip.

**Check on theme park dog kennels.**

Some theme parks, such as Six Flags Fiesta Texas, offer free kennels for park guests; others like Dollywood have low-cost kennels (in this case, *Doggywood*!) for visitors to use.

Although park kennels don't permit overnight boarding, you'll be able to check in your dog for the entire day as you enjoy the park—and you can come back and walk and feed your dog anytime during the day. Check with your theme park on its specific policies; some require a reservation for kennel facilities and some do not.

**Pack plenty of food and treats.**

Be sure to pack plenty of your dog's typical food; not only will this prevent any tummy upsets but you'll also save money by being able to buy the food in your hometown at the store you know has the best prices rather than running around new town looking for a pet supply store!

**Pack an old shower curtain as a seat cover for wet dogs.**

Whether you're traveling in your car or a rented car, keeping the seats free from beach sand and muddy paw prints is a must. You'll find many commercial seat covers available but a low-cost option is a used shower curtain!

# Helping Others

What will you do with all the money you've saved on your own pet's care? Or what if you are currently "between dogs" but feel the need to help other pets or pet parents in need? A myriad of organizations make it easy to contribute.

By offering your time, money, or just by sharing your love of animals, you can be instrumental in improving the pet community as a whole. And, you'll feel a lot better about yourself, too—what a deal!

**Check nonprofits before donating.**

One part of saving money is to make sure the money you do spend is spent wisely—and that includes your donations, whether financial or your volunteer efforts, to animal welfare nonprofits.

You'll find several sites that offer information on nonprofits. *GreatNonprofits.org* is sort of a TripAdvisor-type site for nonprofits filled with reader experiences. We recently took place in a press effort to publicize their Animal Welfare Campaign which sought experiences both good and bad with animal-related nonprofits.

Some other sites to check are Guidestar.org (*www2.guidestar.org*) with reader reviews and *CharityNavigator.org*, which evaluates the financial health of the largest charities.

**Help dogs with a click of your mouse.**

One way to help homeless pets that won't impact your own budget at all is by taking part in one (or all!) of the several online projects that, through their own advertising sponsorship, provide food donations to deserving shelters. Some allow you to set up daily reminders to nudge you to make that daily click!

- **www.freekibble.com and www.freekibblekat.com** Each daily click provides 10 pieces of kibble to animal shelters to help feed dogs (*freekibble.com*) or cats (*freekibblekat.com*). Not only will you feel good for visiting these sites, but you'll have fun, too. Every day, a different trivia question comes up in Bow Wow Trivia and Meow Trivia; click on an answer (right or wrong) and you've donated! Think 10 pieces doesn't sound like too much? Since June 1, 2008, FreeKibble has donated 3.6 million meals to dogs and cats! These sites were

148

created by Mimi Ausland at the age of 12, proving that, regardless of age or resources, we all can do something important to help homeless animals!

- **www.theanimalrescuesite.com** A partner of Petfinder.com, daily clicks on this site go to provide food and care for homeless animals. You can set up daily reminders to email you a note that it's time to make a click or join the Facebook fan page and get a reminder with your news feed.

- **Pets.care2.com** When you click on the "Click to Help" button daily, your click goes to The Humane Society of the United States' (HSUS) Rural Area Veterinary Services program; 100 percent of that donation goes to help spay and neuter, vaccinate, and provide checkups. The pets section is just one part of Care2, with 350 nonprofit partners and 9.4 million members.

**Help shelters with office parties and showers.**

Whether you're planning an office party, a school party, or a holiday party in your home, you can share the fun with needy animals in shelters:

- Consider a dog food drive, dog toy drive, etc. Each guest brings pet food, toys, bedding, etc. to your party, all destined for your local shelter. (Isn't this better than receiving yet another hostess gift you don't really need?)

- In lieu of gift exchanges, consider donations in the name of your office or social group to your local shelter.

- Consider a donation jar at your party to raise money for Kuranda dog and cat beds to keep animals off cold concrete shelter floors during the winter months. By donating through their program at *kuranda.com/donate*, your guests' money will go about 30 percent further than just buying beds and donating them. You'll be able to specify which shelter will receive your donated beds.

- Call your local shelter and ask about their holiday needs. Do they need canned dog food? Bedding? Cleaning supplies? Include a wish list in your holiday invitation and explain to guests you'll have a donation box for goodies.

- Ask yourself if your family really wants to do a gift exchange this holiday or if everyone would like to spend the money on a donation in the family's name to a local shelter or rescue. Especially for adult families, removing the pressure of gift shopping from the holidays can be a real stress reliever and the good feeling you'll receive from knowing you helped homeless animals will be a true gift to yourself!

**Donate through your online purchases.**

Several online portals allow you to click through from their site to some of your favorite merchants' sites, resulting in a donation for each of your online purchases but at no extra costs to you.

Take a moment before you go to an online store to check sites like *www.igive.com* and *www.goodsearch.com*.

**Help animals with your searches.**

By just doing your searches through particular sites, you can donate to animal welfare charities at no cost to you. Sites such as *DoGreatGood.com* and *www.goodsearch.com* donate to animal welfare and other charities. For more, search for "charity search engines."

**Help pet food banks.**

A growing number of pet food banks or pet food pantries offer assistance and want to help. If you need assistance, even for a short time, check with local organizations in your area.

Below you'll find web sites that list pet food pantries (and some that include veterinary assistance, too). Don't see one in your area? Check with your local pet service providers—veterinary clinics, local shelters and rescue organizations—for their recommendations and ask human food pantries if they offer pet food and supplies to their clients.

You'll find information on pet food banks at these sites:

- **Humane Society of the United States**, *www.humanesociety.org* The Humane Society of the United States has an extensive list, divided by state, of local pet food banks. On this site, you'll also find an extensive list of organizations that can assist with veterinary costs.

- **Save Our Pets Food Bank**, *www.saveourpetsfoodbank.org* This Atlanta organization offers services for the region but it has also worked to compile a national list of pet food banks.

- **United Animal Nations**, *www.uan.org* United Animal Nations has a wide variety of assistance organizations listed by location; along with some organizations offering food assistance, you'll find veterinary assistance, financing assistance, and more.

**Help your dog park save money.**

Dog parks are a great resource for dog lovers but they aren't free to operate. One way to help your dog park save money is by bringing your own bags--whether that means reusing plastic

151

grocery bags or bringing inexpensive sandwich bags--rather than using the city-supplied waste bags.

**Help your shelter by donating your time.**

When money's in tight supply, you can still help out your local shelter by giving your time and expertise. Talk with your shelter and see how you can help by photographing dogs, socializing and training dogs, walking dogs, taking dogs to rescue events, and more.

Fostering dogs is another excellent way to help and costs can be minimal and some rescues can help with the cost of dog food.

**Pay it forward with coupons.**

Recently at the pet supply store, the nicest woman in front of us, also buying the same brand, looked back and saw we had a jumbo sack. She asked if it was the 26-pound sack. It was. Saying she couldn't use this because she always bought the smaller sacks, she handed us a $5 coupon!

From there, we ran to the grocery store to pick up a few things for the weekend including some cat litter. While we were in the cat section, we noticed some kind shopper had slipped a couple of random coupons underneath a sack of cat food and some cat treats. It wasn't a store effort, just a simple act of kindness.

Which got us thinking: we cut out coupons from the paper every Sunday anyway…why not cut out the ones we don't need but someone else could use? A great way to help fellow pet lovers–without spending a dime yourself–is to pass along those unused coupons. Just the simple act of cutting out a coupon and tucking it under a pet product can both boost someone's budget and bring some joy to a pet. In these tough economic times, we pet lovers have to stick together!

**Use coupons to help your shelter.**

What can you do with these unused cat/dog food and treat coupons? Take a couple to the store with you each trip and make a purchase for your local shelter. Keep a box in your pantry, add your purchase to the box, and when the box gets full, drop it by your local shelter.

Your donation will make a dog or cat very happy and ease the strains on a shelter budget in these tough times. You can make that coupon go even further by shopping on double coupon day (if your store offers one) or by combining the manufacturer's coupon with a store coupon.

# How Dogs Save You Money

There's no denying it: dogs cost money. But the payback from pooches is something that just can't be measured...or can it? Studies have shown that people with dogs are generally healthier, both physically and mentally.

Recently we interviewed Dr. Mehmet Oz, host of "The Dr. Oz Show" and a big pet lover, about some of the human health benefits dogs provide. According to Dr. Oz:

> "Pets are one of the best excuses to get the physical activity that so many Americans fall down on the job on...."

celebrity tip

"You know people who are heavy often have heavy pets – and the same criteria that you use to get the pet to lose a little bit of that extra fat around the bones of their rib cage are the things that you need to do to lose that fat around your waist."

Besides the healthy influence dogs play on our diet and activity level, Dr. Oz explained to us that getting out and walking your dog can help get you going and set the tone for the entire day by setting your circadian rhythms.

From those health benefits to social benefits, dogs are a definite boon in hard times. Dog owners are finding that when the going gets tough, the tough go play with their dogs! Here are nine ways Rover just might be your answer to the recession:

- **He's a Good Reason to Stay Home.** Staying home—rather then heading out and spending money—is never more appealing than when there's a four-legged friend waiting for you. Suddenly there's a good reason to dine at home or to choose an afternoon at the dog park rather than the shopping mall.

- **He's a Great Exercise Partner.** Need to save money by cutting back on a fitness club membership? No problem. You'll never have a more dedicated personal trainer than your dog who will remind you—and remind you, and remind you—that it is time to get out and exercise.

- **He Loves Day Trips.** Can't afford that week at a Caribbean resort? Fido's happy you're staying home and considering taking him on a day trip to the lake or local park.

- **He Doesn't Mind Cutbacks.** OK, you might not want to opt for a home haircut for yourself, but your dog doesn't mind if you cut out the groomer and just give him a trim yourself.

- **He's Happy with Used Items.** Do the kids want the latest toys in the stores? You won't have that same pressure from your dog. He's happy with used toys from garage sales and thrift stores, perfect for playing fetch or romping around the yard.

- **He's a Great Stress Reliever.** Economic problems cause stress, there's no doubt about it. But it's a proven fact that dogs are an excellent stress reliever and also do wonders to lower high blood pressure. One look in those big eyes and it's easy to see why.

- **He'll Help You Get Out and About.** Whether you've lost your job and no longer see your usual crowd of people or you've just cut back on social events, economic difficulties can mean less social interaction. Your dog, by encouraging you to get out and walk or to play in dog parks, helps you to interact with people who have similar interests.

- **He Knows You Are King.** A beleaguered bank account or a pink slip can leave you feeling worthless. All you have to do, though, is look in your dog's eyes and you know that you're the best there is. You are the center of his world.

- **He Knows the Best Things in Life are Free.** Your dog values your companionship more than anything in the world. Money doesn't mean a thing to him, but you do. There's no greater gift you can give your dog than your own time.

# Appendix A: Dog Food Companies

It pays to get social with dog companies. By subscribing to their e-newsletters, following them on Facebook and Twitter, and checking their website regularly, you can often obtain valuable coupons and coupon codes. Another option is to write directly to the companies and request coupons or free samples. Here's a list of many dog food companies:

Artemis, *www.artemiscompany.com*
The Robert Abady Dog Food Co., *therobertabadydogfoodcoltd.com*

Bench and Field, *www.benchandfield.com*
Bil-Jac, *www.bil-jac.com*
Blackwood Pet Food, *www.blackwoodpetfood.com*
Blue Buffalo, *bluebuff.com*
Blue Seal, *www.blueseal.com*

Bravo! Raw Diets, *bravorawdiet.com*
Breeder's Choice Pet Foods, *breeders-choice.com*
Burns Pet Health, *www.burnspethealth.com*

California Natural, *www.naturapet.com*
Canidae All-Natural Pet Foods, *canidae.com*
Canine Caviar, *www.caninecaviar.com*
Castor & Pollux, *www.castorpolluxpet.com*
Cesar Canine Cuisine, *www.cesar.com*
Champion Petfoods, *www.championpetfoods.com*
Chicken Soup for the Pet Lover's Soul,
*chickensoupforthepetloverssoul.com*
Cloudstar, *www.cloudstar.com*

DAD'S Pet Foods, *www.dadspetcare.com*
Dogswell, *www.dogswell.com*
Dr. Harvey's, *www.drharveys.com*
Dynamite Marketing, *www.dynamitemarketing.com*

Eagle Pack, *eaglepack.com*
Eukanuba, *www.eukanuba.com*
Evanger's Dog and Cat Food Company, *www.evangersdogfood.com*
EVO, *www.naturapet.com*
Evolve Pet Foods, *www.evolvepet.com*

Flint River Ranch, *www.frrco.com*
Freshpet Select, *www.homestyleselect.com*
Fromm Family Foods, *www.frommfamily.com*

Grandma Lucy's Diner, *www.grandmalucys.com*

Halo, *www.halopets.com*
Happy Dog Food, *www.happydogfood.com*
Harmony Farms, *harmonypetproducts.com*
HealthWise, *www.naturapet.com*

Healthy Pet Products, *www.healthypetdiet.com*
Hill's Pet Nutrition, *www.hillspet.com*
Holistic Blend, *www.holisticblend.com*
The Honest Kitchen, *www.thehonestkitchen.com*

Iams, *www.iams.com*
Innova, *www.naturapet.com*
Ivet Professional Formula Pet Foods, *www.ivetfoods.com*

Karma Organic Food for Dogs, *www.karmaorganicpet.com*
Kibbles 'n Bits, *www.kibblesnbits.com*

Life's Abundance, *www.healthypetnet.com*

Merrick Pet foods, *www.merrickpetcare.com*
mORIGINS, *www.morigins.com*
Muenster Milling Natural Dog Food, *muenstermilling.com*

Natura, *www.naturapet.com*
Natural Balance Pet Foods, *naturalbalanceinc.com*
Natural Life Nutritional Pet Products, *nlpp.com*
Nature's Logic, *natureslogic.com*
Nature's Recipe, *www.naturesrecipe.com*
Nature's Variety, *www.naturesvariety.com*
Newman's Own Organics, *www.newmansownorganics.com*
Nulo, *www.nulo.com*
Nutro, *www.thenutrocompany.com*

Old Mother Hubbard (treats & biscuits), *www.oldmotherhubbard.com*
Oma's Pride, *www.omaspride.com*

Paw Naturaw, *pawnaturaw.com*
Pedigree, *www.pedigree.com*
Performatrin Ultra, *www.performatrinultra.com*
Petcurean Pet Nutrition, *www.petcurean.com*

PetGuard, *petguard.com*
Pet Promise, *petpromiseinc.com*
PMI Nutrition, *www.pminutrition.com*
Precise Pet Products, *precisepet.com*
Premium Edge Pet Food, *premiumedgepetfood.com*
Primal Pet Foods, *www.primalpetfoods.com*
PRO PAC Superpremium Pet Food, *www.propacpetfood.com*
Professional Pet Foods, *professionalpetfood.com*
Proportions, *www.proportions.com*
Purina, *www.purina.com*
Purina Dog Chow, *www.longliveyourdog.com*
Purina ONE, *www.purinaone.com*
Purina Pro Plan, *www.proplan.com*
Purina Veterinary Diets, *www.purinaveterinarydiets.com*

Royal Canin, *www.royalcanin.us*
Rudy Green's Doggy Cuisine, *www.rudygreens.com*

Skippy, *www.skippydog.com*
Sojos All Natural Dog Food and Treats, *www.sojos.com*
Solid Gold Health Products for Pets, *www.solidgoldhealth.com*
Sportmix, *www.sportmix.com*
Stella and Chewy's, *www.stellaandchewys.com*
Steve's Real Food, *stevesrealfood.com*

Three Dog Bakery, *www.threedog.com*
Tiki Pet Food, *www.petropics.com*
Tuffy's Pet Foods, *www.tuffyspetfoods.com*

VeRUS Pet Foods, *veruspetfoods.com*

Wellness Healthy Dog and Cat Food, *www.wellnesspetfood.com*
Wysong Natural Pet Foods, *www.wysong.net*
Ziwipeak, *ziwipeak.com*

# Appendix B: Prescription & Insurance Websites

## Online Pet Pharmacies

*These pharmacies are each Veterinary-Verified Internet Pharmacy Practice (Vet-VIPPS) Sites; you'll be able to click on a Vet-VIPPS seal on each to be taken to a verification site to check that this site is certified.*

1800PetMeds, *www.1800petmeds.com*
Doctors Foster and Smith, *www.drsfostersmith.com*
PetCare Rx, *www.petcarerx.com*
VetRxDirect, *vetrxdirect.com*

## Pet Insurance—US

24 Pet Watch Insurance, *www.24petwatch.com*
AKC Pet Healthcare Plan, *www.akcpethealthcare.com*
ASPCA (through Hartsfield Group, Inc.), *www.aspcapetinsurance.com*
Embrace Pet Insurance, *www.embracepetinsurance.com*
Hartsfield Pet Health Insurance, *www.hartvillepetinsurance.com*
Healthy Paws Pet Insurance, *www.healthypawspetinsurance.com*
PetFirst Healthcare, *www.petfirsthealthcare.com*
Petplan Pet Health Insurance, *www.gopetplan.com*
Pets Best, *www.petsbest.com*
Petshealth Care Plan (Hartsfield Group), *www.petshealthplan.com*
PurinaCare, *www.purinacare.com*
Trupanion, *www.trupanionpetinsurance.com*
Veterinary Pet Insurance (VPI), *www.petinsurance.com*

## Pet Insurance—Canada

Hbc Pet Insurance, *www.petinsurancehbc.com*
PC Financial Pet Insurance, *www.pcinsurance.ca*
PetCare, *www.petcareinsurance.com*
Petsecure, *www.petsecure.com*
PurinaCare Canada, *www.purinacare.ca*
Vetinsurance (Trupanion), *www.vetinsurance.com*

# Index

# About the Authors

John Bigley and Paris Permenter, a husband-wife team, have authored 27 books ranging from travel guidebooks to cookbooks for Random House, Globe Pequot, Avalon, and more. Their dog articles have appeared in magazines ranging from *Reader's Digest* to local dog publications. Paris and John have appeared as expert guests on numerous television and radio programs.

Lifetime dog lovers, John and Paris launched DogTipper.com in 2008, highlighting tips for dog lovers with additional sections including dog news, dog-centric festivals, celebrity canines, pet product reviews, Dog of the Day, dog rescue, and more. They live with their dogs and cats in the Texas Hill Country near Austin.

6514105R0

Made in the USA
Charleston, SC
02 November 2010